PRAISE FOR
FROM THE GROUND UP

"Noell Jett didn't learn by sitting on the sidelines of life just hoping, dreaming, wishing, or praying (although she did all those things). Noell Jett learned by *doing*; she dug her hands in the dirt and she wasn't afraid to fail. In fact, Noell wasn't afraid of anything. Her hard-earned life lessons are beautifully and powerfully told in *From the Ground Up*. With grit and determination Noell and Daniel overcame seemingly impossible challenges. Their heart-warming story just may inspire you to see life's challenges in a new light."

—JULIE LANCIA AND JODIE KAMMERER, THE DESIGN TWINS

"I first found Noell on TikTok and was immediately captivated by her posts! Noell's story is so inspiring, an absolute must-read! An amazing love story between a family and their home."

—SOPHIE LIARD, THE FOLDING LADY

"I started following Noell because I felt such a parallel to our similarities. Family, Jesus, homeschooling, and creating a home of purpose for those we loved. Her strength and endurance through her hardships has only made her story that much more compelling. She truly represents the American dream and this book empowers all women to be the best they can be."

—RACHEL VAN KLUYVE, AUTHOR OF *SHE MADE HERSELF A HOME*

"Noell is an overcomer and continues to inspire me (and all of her followers) daily. *From the Ground Up is* a timeless story of overcoming insurmountable obstacles and is sure to inspire others to take action and build the life of their dreams."

—SARA MCDANIEL, CREATOR OF @SIMPLYSOUTHERNCOTTAGE

"I just adore Noel! I came across her social media account one day while browsing online and was immediately drawn in to her world. She has overcome so much and has brilliantly harnessed the power of social media to make her dreams come true. Her inspiring story will empower you to stop letting your past hold you back and explore the dreams you've been putting off in your own life. Love this book!"

—ALI FEDOTOWSKY MANNING, BLOGGER
AND SEASON SIX BACHELORETTE

from the
GROUND UP

from the GROUND UP

BUILDING A DREAM HOUSE

—AND A BEAUTIFUL LIFE—

THROUGH GRIT AND GRACE

NOELL JETT

WITH MELISSA FERGUSON

NELSON BOOKS

An Imprint of Thomas Nelson

Published in Nashville, Tennessee, by Nelson Books, an imprint of Thomas Nelson. Nelson Books and Thomas Nelson are registered trademarks of HarperCollins Christian Publishing, Inc.

Thomas Nelson titles may be purchased in bulk for educational, business, fundraising, or sales promotional use. For information, please email SpecialMarkets@ThomasNelson.com.

Any internet addresses, phone numbers, or company or product information printed in this book are offered as a resource and are not intended in any way to be or to imply an endorsement by Thomas Nelson, nor does Thomas Nelson vouch for the existence, content, or services of these sites, phone numbers, companies, or products.

Scripture quotations are taken from the ESV° Bible (The Holy Bible, English Standard Version°). Copyright © 2001 by Crossway, a publishing ministry of Good News Publishers. Used by permission. All rights reserved.

Names and identifying characteristics of some individuals have been changed to preserve their privacy.

Unless otherwise noted, photos are from the author's personal collection.

Library of Congress Cataloging-in-Publication Data

Names: Jett, Noell, 1981- author.
Title: From the ground up: building a dream house-and a beautiful life-through grit and grace / Noell Jett.
Description: Nashville, Tennessee: Nelson Books, [2022] | Summary: "Popular social media star Noell Jett shares the unbelievable story behind her beautiful 3,700-square foot custom farmhouse--built by hand and savvy influencer marketing--and the key strategies she learned while overcoming a difficult past"-- Provided by publisher.
Identifiers: LCCN 2021039676 (print) | LCCN 2021039677 (ebook) | ISBN 9781400230303 (HC) | ISBN 9781400230310 (eBook)
Subjects: LCSH: House construction. | Jett, Noell, 1981---Homes and haunts. | Jett, Noell, 1981---Influence. | Bloggers--United States. | Conduct of life. | Social media--Authorship.
Classification: LCC TH4815.4 .J48 2022 (print) | LCC TH4815.4 (ebook) | DDC 643/.7--dc23
LC record available at https://lccn.loc.gov/2021039676
LC ebook record available at https://lccn.loc.gov/2021039677

Printed in the United States of America

22 23 24 25 26 LSC 10 9 8 7 6 5 4 3 2 1

Contents

CONTENTS

Foreword

by Liz Marie Galvan

*H*ome. It's a word that evokes feelings of safety, warmth, inclusion, coziness, and joy. The ways we build, care for, and live in our homes varies, but one thing remains true: we want our homes to be refuges, made with love and care, no matter the size or budget. Last year when I was struggling to write my book, *Cozy White Cottage Seasons*, my friend, the gorgeous author of this book, Noell Jett, shook me from my thoughts that building, decorating, and making a beautiful home was shallow and frivolous. She reminded me that now, more than ever, our homes are so important. Important for building relationships with our loved ones, important for cultivating a healthy mind and body, and most of all, important for nurturing ourselves, our children, and our family's needs.

Noell has always inspired me with her ideas for creating a beautiful home that she shares on her social media accounts of the Jett Sett Farmhouse, but those images are not all there is to her story. In *From the Ground Up*, she gives us a behind-the-scenes view of the deep, riveting obstacles she had to overcome to build that amazing dream home.

In a culture of social media snapshots and highlight reels, it's easy to fall into the trap of thinking we're the only ones with struggles, heartaches, or piles of dirty laundry. The reality? We all have past and current struggles, we all have bad days, we all have trials to overcome. We are not seeing the full, 24-hour surveillance video of each other's lives. After my husband and I endured years of infertility and miscarriages, we adopted our son, Copeland. While we continued to share pictures of our cozy house projects and life online, behind the scenes, I was soaking in our new baby, changing diapers and doing feedings while not getting sleep, and nobody knew.

In the pages of this book, Noell reminds all of us that the feeling of home is a gift that not everyone is afforded. Some of us have to claw, crawl, and courageously fight the hardest battles for that feeling. It doesn't happen overnight but after many battles lost and, finally, won. Cozy isn't a birthright, but Noell shows us all that home, family, and love are possible if we don't give up and if we keep our faith and hope alive no matter how long and painful the journey.

Get cozy, snuggle up, and be prepared to be inspired by Noell's journey and motivated to fight for the life you want no matter what hurdles may come your way.

—*Liz Marie Galvan, interior designer, blogger, shop owner,*
and author of Cozy White Cottage Seasons

Introduction

YOU CAN TURN A
NO INTO A YES

I can't put a number on the times I've shared about my home and life on social media and someone has commented, "Must be nice to be rich."

Yes, I live in a beautiful, 3,700-square-foot, custom-built modern farmhouse.

Yes, I have been blessed with the opportunity to make thousands of dollars posting on social media by collaborating with companies and brands I believe in.

Yes, my account has been featured by *Better Homes and Gardens*, the *Farmhouse Movement*, *Tennessean*, and a dozen other publications.

But that is a far cry from my life just four years ago, and my entire lifetime before that. While my parents were hardworking, I grew up with seven people in a 1,200-square-foot house with missing windowpanes, only one woodburning fireplace to fight the bitter-cold Missouri winters, and just a few rotten boards away from being condemned. I endured the dizzying effects of a childhood in a religious cult and the struggle of separating truth from falsehood as an adult. I essentially started supporting myself at age sixteen, and at one point worked four retail jobs, averaging sixty-five hours a week to pay the bills.

My life wasn't a breeze then, and the fact is, it still isn't now. No, what we have now is hard work multiplied by the blessing of a successful brand.

Together, my husband, Daniel, and I built our house by hand with almost no experience. Almost every screw, every nail, every piece of lumber came from our family working together to get it done. We had a dream to make this home for ourselves, and even without the funds to pull it off, even with family, friends, and total strangers telling us we couldn't do it, we committed to the plan.

Why did I sign up for such a wild dream? Because I'd lived through enough experiences—generational poverty, single motherhood, multiple miscarriages, chronic depression, illness, and abuse—that I'd learned how to overcome. I'd learned how to say yes when the world said no and how to persevere when the going gets tough—or starts tough. And I knew, when it was the right thing to do, how to take a leap of faith.

In March 2018 we had just closed on the loan for our house. We didn't have the money to make our home anything fancy; Daniel and I ran a small business while I also homeschooled our children. Funds were tight. We were relying on our plan to purchase as many items for the house secondhand and to do as much of the building ourselves as possible—making it a truly DIY home. There would be no general contractor in hand. There would be no subcontractors going in and out. I was never going to be that woman waltzing into the jobsite with a cup of coffee in hand, checking on the progress of the crews before heading out, manicured nails intact.

As much as possible it would be just us, and we were going to take as long as necessary to get the house finished. Five years. Ten. It didn't matter because this was our dream.

As we buckled down and began the process, we had the air knocked out of us time and time again by the high estimates. Framing materials were going to be $50,000. Not to mention the framer himself, who was going to charge $40,000 to put up those materials.

Those two estimates alone were going to cost a third of our entire limited budget. It was staggering.

But on July 5, 2018, something incredible happened. We received an email from a door company saying that they were launching their company and were looking for a family building a modern farmhouse in Florida with whom to collaborate. They'd stumbled across the Instagram account I'd made only five months earlier, @jettsetfarmhouse, and thought our home was exactly what they were looking for. In fact, not only did they want to partner with us; they wanted to give us *every gorgeous, high-quality door* we wanted for our home in exchange for a few pictures on social media—a collaboration that ended up being worth over $70,000.

It was at this moment everything changed.

Daniel and I realized that if we changed the lens through which we viewed our plans, if we created a brand, if we utilized social media, we just might be able to not only expedite building our dream home but end up with a product far greater than we could have achieved with our limited funds. And as it turned out, we ended up getting that and so much more.

Our home is more than just a pretty white farmhouse. For me, it represents a lifetime of facing challenges and fighting through them, of making plans but pivoting when needed. For Daniel and me, and our four children, it means countless hours of working side by side as a family to build something we believed in.

Everybody has dreams. Challenges. Past hardships and hopes for the future. And in this book, I want to share with you my stories. Not just of how I overcame my past, but of how I came to love my life, build a home I adore, and grow a career on my own terms. I want to share tips and tricks on how you can not only build your own dream house, regardless of budget, but also mend a broken relationship or build a brand from nothing.

I want to help you chase your dreams.

Come join me.

Chapter 1

RICH OR POOR

It wasn't long ago that I was sitting cross-legged in my garage, surrounded by cardboard boxes full of memories. Not my own memories, but those belonging to my husband. Boxes full of baseball mitts and medals, science projects and T-shirts so beloved they were swallowed up in holes. While sorting I came across a single piece of paper dated from his high school years. An essay titled "Three Dreams for My Life."

One. Daniel wanted to get married.

Two. He wanted to have lots of kids.

Three. He wanted to build his own house.

I smiled because that was so . . . Daniel. Professing to himself and others even at such a young age that *this life*, the one we are living right now, fulfilled his dreams. His goal wasn't to become a millionaire or retire at twenty-five so he could travel the world. Not to head off to an Ivy League school or make his own music album. No, his dreams were aspirational and yet humble at the same time.

He wanted me.

He wanted our children.

And he wanted to build the floor beneath me with his own hands.

And didn't he just do exactly that? Despite the blind curves and miles of chugging uphill on empty, didn't we do it all together?

None of this came easy. Not the health of our marriage, not the blessing of our children, and certainly not our house. But if my childhood in poverty taught me one thing, it was that if I wanted something, I couldn't just pedal slowly toward it and assume it would turn out all right. No, if I wanted something and I felt the call to move toward it, I had to *fight for it* with everything in me.

My childhood was not spent in affluence. My four brothers and I didn't wear designer labels—we didn't even know what the inside of a shopping mall looked like. My mother didn't use colorful silicone dividers to slide kiwi slices and sushi into our sleek lunch boxes to take to school. We didn't jump into the family minivan for grand skiing getaways in Colorado.

No, our lives were the opposite. We were the kids who didn't have money for pizza when going on class field trips. The kids who never went to the doctor or dentist. Instead of hearing from our mother, "All right, kids, it's time for your yearly checkup," we were told, "God has given you healthy bodies and good teeth, so we never have to go." Instead of spending our weekends at the soccer fields, we were in the woods, cutting down cedar trees to sell to the sawmill to help make ends meet.

Growing up in poverty was an all-consuming experience. Because I lived in a home steeped in a religion that believed women largely belonged at home instead of in the workplace, that the harboring of money was evil, and that it was unacceptable to trust or accept any financial assistance from the government, we always had *just* enough, but not an inch more. It wasn't that my parents couldn't make money. No, the problem was that our church's extremist beliefs hamstrung my family from keeping anything beyond basic clothes and staple meals.

We didn't need to replace those broken doors and windowpanes to keep the chickens from wandering onto our beds at night.

Or patch the roof to keep flurries from drifting onto our faces while we slept.

And so, despite my father's hardworking labors—whether as a bricklayer, or a sawmill worker, or a pastor, we never achieved a place of true stability. But living beneath the poverty line meant that a family as large as ours struggled.

The lack of funds affected not just our physical circumstances but also our emotions. It colored our world with an anxiety other children in different economic circumstances didn't see or understand. That anxiety, that stress, was laid upon us every hour of every day. Our goal was survival.

When I was fourteen, my first cyst burst. I was in my room, changing clothes, and immediately fell to my knees in immense pain far worse than anything I'd ever experienced. It felt like I had been stabbed in the gut with a knife. We didn't know at the time that I had endometriosis, but we did know something was terribly wrong.

When my parents realized the situation was serious enough to seek medical attention, they packed me into our beat-up diesel Suburban, and we began the twenty-minute trek from our country house to the hospital. This was a big deal because there were only a handful of times in my childhood that one of us had been sick enough or injured enough for our parents to consider medical care. Once was when my youngest brother broke his arm, and even then they waited three days to take him to the county health clinic— where the doctor nearly turned my mother in to child protective services because she had waited so long.

When my brother had appendicitis, my dad responded by making him get out of bed and go to work mowing the forty to fifty lawns he was responsible for in his lawn-mowing service. Told him he needed to "man up" and work through the pain. My brother ended up having an appendectomy just in time.

We were taught to carefully analyze the situation for any way around medical care to avoid the expense. Even when my dad got seriously injured in a lawn-mowing accident, we didn't immediately call 911. No, instead he lay there, paralyzed from the neck down, asking me questions like, "Am I bleeding anywhere?" as he tried to work out whether or not treating his would-be-permanent injury was worth the cost of the medical services.

When my cyst burst, instead of fearing for myself and my well-being, do you know what absolutely terrified me on that drive to the hospital?

The all-consuming fear?

The medical bill.

This was two years after the accident that left my dad a partial paraplegic, managing to walk again and do some tasks but ultimately all while feeling nothing but nerve pain from the neck down. We were still paying off medical bills from his months of hospitalization. We didn't have health insurance and needed to avoid any additional costs.

People who don't live in severe poverty just can't understand that feeling, that fear. They don't know just how intense my terror was when I lost a ten-dollar bill as a young girl. They don't know that exact wash of relief I felt when I finally found it tucked in the bottom of my shoe. In our family, every *single* penny was precious, and it was our job to do everything we could to help shoulder the family burden. My brothers and I worked *hard* doing anything we could to help: picking stones from fields for five dollars per container, cleaning houses, mowing lawns, selling cards and gift wrap.

And in that moment, as the cyst lay ruptured in my abdomen,

the thought of *adding* to that financial strain instead of helping to alleviate it was more painful than what was happening in my body.

During that ride I sat in the back seat, clutching my waist, trying to will away the pain. Terrified of causing my family even more financial stress. Summoning everything within me in a desperate plea to *just make it all go away.*

And sure enough, five minutes out from the hospital, I threw up, and the pain cleared (unlike just a few short years later, when another cyst burst and I almost lost my life). I vividly remember holding my breath, waiting, listening to my body. Then, when at last sure, saying, "Pull over. I think I'm okay."

So we did.

With a collective sigh of relief, we did.

Not because my parents weren't worried about me. Not because they weren't terrified seeing their only daughter hunched over in pain and having no idea what was wrong. No. They turned around for the same reason I begged them to: because they were just as scared of the financial consequences as they were of my sudden illness. And in our world, if there was even a sliver of an opportunity to escape medical treatment, you did. Always.

This is what poverty does to you. It shackles you. It makes you drag those fears and anxieties around every day while you go to school, eat meals, play games. Makes you face demons on the inside all while looking like the average kid playing ball on the outside.

Poverty brings chaos.

And after growing up in poverty, I realized I had two choices. I could let myself live the rest of my life in the chaos, eventually bearing children and letting them grow up the same way, or I could do everything within my power to break out. I could fight and claw so hard that no matter what happened at the end of the day, whether I

ultimately failed or succeeded, I'd know that I'd tried my hardest—
and for that I could hold my head up high.

So I chose to fight.

And in fighting, I learned lessons applicable not just to overcoming generational poverty but to how Daniel and I would build
our farmhouse—and life: from the ground up. Lessons that are
applicable to all who are trying to push beyond their particular
circumstances. That includes you, whether you are trying to
provide a better life for your children or gain peace of mind for
yourself.

Make a Declaration and Stick to It

The harsh realities of my childhood were the building blocks giving
me the determination to do whatever it took to get out of tough
situations—which, quite frankly, would come in handy more often
during our farmhouse build than I would have ever imagined
possible. I learned early on that if I wanted to get out of poverty, I
was going to have to work, and work *hard*. Work creatively. Be willing to stumble and fall flat on my face and get up and take the next
step. And, in worst-case scenarios, be willing to press on alone even
if no one believed in me. Even if I had no one's support financially,
emotionally, or otherwise.

In my determination I worked so hard that I graduated early
from our little church school when I was sixteen. And instead of
stopping there, I pushed onward.

College.

I qualified for Pell Grants, which covered most of the tuition for
a local Bible college. I had a car because a lady I cleaned for in high
school had financed the $2,500 and I had worked hard to pay it off

while cleaning in the afternoons and evenings and on weekends. And once I entered Bible college, which trained people for ministry, I juggled four retail jobs, working every single free moment outside church and school for a total of sixty-five hours a week. At six dollars an hour, this gave me enough money to afford gas, food, insurance, and clothes.

A year later, a new Bible college opened up in Oklahoma City that aligned more closely with my family's strict religious beliefs, so my parents forced me to transfer there. I did, finding more work to keep myself going.

My life was *incredibly* busy, but I was doing it. I was getting out of poverty.

I was succeeding.

And then a wrench was thrown into my life, disguised as a serendipitous surprise: I met my first love.

With such little experience with the world outside my childhood home and the extremist church in which I'd been raised, I fell and I fell *hard*.

He bought the ring. We planned on getting married. But when he changed his mind and broke my heart, I dropped out of college and went back to the only place I felt I could: home. And suddenly I looked around and realized I had fallen back into the trap I was trying to escape. I never anticipated that first love coming into— and departing—my life so quickly, and it shook me up. And frankly, I could've used the whole experience as an excuse to wallow and retire my dreams. The boy broke my heart. *I* was doing great until *he* showed up and ruined everything.

Or . . . I could press past it. Move on.

I still wanted more from life. I wanted out of the poverty I faced. I wanted to succeed. I would keep going.

But making that decision to leave my childhood home and world brought another unanticipated hurdle. Now that I was back in my old world, there were people in my life who didn't want me to go. They didn't think I could make it out there in the big world or—given the religious extremism I faced—that it was right for me as a woman to try.

But I forced myself to do it. I packed up my things and what meager resources I had and started my life over again—this time at another Bible college in a different state and in a different world. It wasn't easy to get back on track. In fact, it was much harder than it would have been had I never derailed in the first place, but I'd made a declaration. I couldn't go home and give up on my goal of breaking free from the generational poverty that bound me. I wanted out. I had to stick to my plan.

I learned in that experience how imperative it is not to be afraid to disappoint people around you, even if no one understands or agrees with what you see for yourself. Just as there were many times in our house build when people doubted us or disagreed with our choices, I knew I couldn't live to please other people. I couldn't be afraid to make my own choices for my own life.

Be Willing to Face Failure

I could've let the mistakes during my first year of college determine the path for the rest of my life. I could've told myself, "You were a fool for falling for that guy, and you're a fool still for trying to leave. Who were you kidding?"

Instead I had to swallow the temptation to feel ashamed of or embarrassed by my mistakes and accept them. So I messed up. So I failed. You know what? That's okay. That's normal. Instead of letting it get me down, I used it as an opportunity for a fresh start. I chose not to be embarrassed by failure. I focused on learning from my mistakes and using those lessons to better my life.

Even during our house build, we faced failures more times than we could count. Just finding land took seven years. *Seven years.* Hour after hour, day after day, we'd drive around, hunting for that perfect little spot of land. Living in the St. Augustine area, we knew that land was hard to come by, and often once you found it, the land had already been sold.

Then one day I spotted a lot for sale and mentioned it as an aside to Daniel, already knowing we wouldn't want it because it didn't have any trees and was in a low-lying area prone to flooding. We made the drive out there anyway, just to be certain, and sure enough, Daniel agreed that the lot wasn't worth pursuing. *But*, he said, he did notice the fully treed, vacant lot at the end of that same road. There was no For Sale sign, but that wouldn't stop us.

We looked up the owners' information on the county website and drafted a letter, asking if they would be willing to sell us the land. The very next day Daniel called me. When I answered, he asked if he could stop by and talk to the owners. I remember how I said, "They're either going to love you or shoot you, so talk fast!" And sure enough, they agreed to sell!

After so many years of searching, we were elated. We drafted and dropped off the contract a few days later, energy and expectations high.

But then, nothing.

Two painfully long weeks went by, and we got a text: they had changed their minds.

That victorious moment of *finally* finding our dream acre and a half, contacting the owners, negotiating the deal, getting the handshake agreement, and working up a contract . . . all for nothing.

More failure. More waiting.

We could've given up then. Dropped our long-held dream. It'd been, after all, seven years.

But instead we kept hunting, kept our eyes peeled, and kept waiting. After another six months my husband—unbeknownst to me—again reached out to the land owners. Just quietly checked in one last time to see if they might be willing to sell, hoping that he might be able to surprise me with the greatest of presents just before Christmas, which also happens to be my birthday. And this time they agreed.

It took several years of failures to get that one win, but oh, what a win.

Dream Big

I vividly remember sitting in my little cubicle at our church school as a child, daydreaming about something bigger. While I wasn't sure what that looked like exactly, I felt constricted in my life and felt the dream, the *wish* for something more.

I lived such a sheltered life, spending all my time either at home or at the small church that served as our school during the week, with no idea people could live differently than me. My daydreams never included money, as I didn't realize having much money was a possibility. However, I knew the chaos and anxiety my family lived in. I saw how exhausted and stressed both of my parents were. I knew I wanted an orderly, calm, chaos-free life where I wasn't constantly worried about money, where I wasn't stealing communion bread out of the church freezer or cookies from the children's church stash because I was hungry.

I wanted to be a mother one day who wasn't so strapped for cash that after driving her kids to school she had to wait on the property

Some dreams are worth giving it all you've got.

for hours just so she didn't have to spend gas money on a thirty-minute drive home and back.

I wanted to buy real fruit from the grocery store, instead of always and *only* picking pieces from thorny trees and bushes. I wanted my children to know the taste of an avocado, yogurt, or simply a banana before they were full-grown. I wanted to be able to afford gas heat, instead of boiling water on a stove to pour in a bathtub for all seven family members to take turns sharing.

If I ever managed my own garden, I'd do it for the enjoyment instead of forcing my whole family, young children included, to labor heavily so we could have enough vegetables to can or freeze for the year. If I ever hunted, I'd do it because eating meat from the kill was just the prize at the end of a long day, instead of hunting being our only source of meat aside from the cows, chickens, and pigs we raised and slaughtered. I wanted to buy new clothes rather than owning the hideous culottes and hand-me-down dresses I was required to wear.

When I had children someday, I did not want them to experience the stress and fears that I faced. I didn't know exactly what I was dreaming for, but the hope to live a different life was so strong that it carried me through my darkest days. And now that I stand where I am today, I wish I could go back and tell that little girl she would one day achieve far more than her little sheltered mind could fathom.

Maybe that's where you are. Maybe you can't even write down specifically what you want because all you know is you want something *different* from what you have now. Some dreams are worth giving it all you've got. Why not yours?

Chapter 2

WHEN THE GOING GETS ROUGH

My tank top is slick with sweat as I raise my machete yet again to hack through the underbrush. We're new owners of only an acre and a half of land, and yet the foliage is so thick and the land so full of scrub oaks, palmettos, pines, water oaks, and live oaks that I can't see more than five feet in front of me. I clear one foot at a time as I take a step forward. For six more weeks Daniel and I will battle our way into our treasured land to make a path for our future home.

It's only April, and yet the Florida heat beats down mercilessly. I take a hand off my machete long enough to bat away the flies dancing around my brow and then raise my machete again. Even through the work and despite the exhaustion, I can't help but be grateful, keenly aware of the far cry my current life is from my childhood.

Of how far I've come.

As a young girl, on Sunday mornings I used to sit straight in the pew and try my best not to itch at the neck of my hand-me-down polyester dress. On the outside the building looked like any normal church. Cars in the parking lot. A modern church sign facing the road beckoning people in. Men in suits and ties at the doors, smiling as they wait for the final stragglers to rush their children inside.

Meanwhile, the pastor would wipe at the sheen on his damp forehead—but his sweat was for reasons far different from physical exercise. He preached with enthusiasm: "And let us not deceive ourselves into forgetting the abomination it is when girls walk around, proudly displaying their shoulders, or violate their gender by putting on slacks as though men. For as the good Lord says, 'The woman shall not wear that which pertaineth unto a man, neither shall a man put on a woman's garment: for all that do so are abomination unto the LORD thy God.' God did *not* call the female gender to violate the temples that are their bodies in such a way. God did *not* bring you into the world to prostitute yourselves with your bodies instead of working quietly with kind and humble hearts. Remember," he added, peering down at the few of us in the room, *"slits are for sluts."*

I sat between my parents and brothers, knees pressed firmly together, dress puddling around my well-worn black shoes. The pastor opened up for a time of prayer. And I, like my mother and every female in the congregation, bowed my head silently. Because of course we were not allowed to pray in church in the presence of men.

For the first seventeen years of my existence, until the day my family was excommunicated, this church was my whole life. Restrained from forming relationships with anyone outside of our small congregation, because anyone outside of our specific church was "wicked." Sternly told time and time again that the government was evil, frightening us as children with declarations that the Department of Children's Services was there only to steal us from our parents. Making us believe that if we ever called the police, they would brutally strip us from our loved ones. All matters were to be privately settled in our church, and the police were to be left out; otherwise you and your family could face excommunication.

The rules were constant, at times bizarre, and never to be questioned.

To go swimming anywhere, which meant in a lake, river, or creek, I had to be fully clothed and only in the company of my immediate family or other women. If a man happened to drive by, all the women had to duck under the water until he had passed.

As if the constant services weren't enough, parents were told that their children needed to attend the school at the church or else they would fall into the same reckless, vile lifestyles as those in the world. Yet they were also required to pay a tuition for each of their children to attend. For families like mine, with several children and little income, this meant scraping to get over $150 *per* child *per* month, not including workbooks, to attend a nonaccredited school that taught through fear and silence.

Once a youth in our church who attended public school died in a car crash. In the receiving line at the funeral, the pastor declared loudly to another family that unless they put their children back in his school, they would be the next to end up in a casket. Because, clearly, the contemptible sin of attending public school was the reason God had taken that child from this world.

My parents, as afraid and manipulated as the others, wanted the best for us, so they sacrificed what little money they had. Only this is what my school life looked like:

No talking was allowed, and by that I mean nearly no communication whatsoever. From eight thirty in the morning until three thirty in the afternoon, excluding two short recesses and lunch, I'd sit at my desk in silence. The teacher, who rarely possessed a college degree, sat at a desk at the front of the classroom and walked around in the morning while we silently filled out a goal chart for the day. Once they checked our goals, they'd return to their desk and we would sit at ours for the rest of the day, working silently through our workbooks.

Dividers separated me from other students. If I had a question for the teacher, I placed the American or Christian flag on my desk and waited for them to arrive. When I completed a quiz I'd walk to the center of the room and score my own work, go back to my seat to rework answers if I got anything wrong, and go back to score again until I got it right. And if I made a mistake while grading—as was the case for me *often* with my attention-deficit disorder—the teacher would automatically call me a cheater, at times resulting in a paddling at school, followed by a switching at home.

And while that particular broken, unhealthy, and unbiblical institution did hold me down for years, it didn't break me in the end. Though it took several years to unravel the mess they'd made of my mind—a thousand knotted questions to work through about identity, life, and truth—I did finally get out. And that experience taught me a thing or two when it came time to become independent. Eventually, it even helped me build our house.

I'm a Strong Woman—and That Is Good

My entire childhood was spent under the hovering message that I was second-rate. Men were the ones to speak. To give orders. To work. To direct the women and children.

The men were the ones who lived without rules.

Women and girls were to keep silent. They were the ones to dutifully serve their husbands and masters. They were the ones to quit their jobs the moment they bore children, to instead make it their life's work to keep the bowl of bean dip full and casseroles in the oven, to wait quietly in the corner with a smile on their faces. They were the ones blamed if or when men stumbled sexually. They were the ones whose intellect was doubted for every decision.

In my little classroom in kindergarten, my first coursework outlined that women were to be subservient to men, that men were revered and superior to women. From such a young age that my toes didn't even reach the ground as I sat in my chair, I heard the messages over and over: The role of a wife was to unquestioningly obey her husband through submission. Girls were shameful and disgusting if they revealed the same body parts boys did, such as shoulders and knees. The only place a woman belonged was the home—unless, in carefully reviewed instances and under the approval of the men in their lives, they taught children in Christian schools or were secretaries under men's direction. Without question I was under the authority of my father for however many years it took me to marry—even if I was fifty years old—at which point he would hand the reins over to my spouse.

For two decades I lived with that message hammered into my ears, feeling like a failure every time I spoke up, every time I demonstrated courage, every time I even desired something besides what I was "supposed" to be as a woman. I can't even count how many times I was told my heart was not submissive because I begged my father to allow me to get bangs (cutting hair was not allowed) or wear a real swimsuit (when any truly good Christian girl wouldn't even ask such a vile thing) or resented my father telling me I had to forfeit a pair of pajama pants somebody had given me (because he wanted to be able to stand at the pulpit and say that his only daughter didn't own a single pair of pants).

I was supposed to be happy. Quiet. Submissive. I was supposed to be that good little girl whose aspirations never veered from marrying a rising pastor and raising his young.

But I wanted more things. Different things.

Until one day something horrible happened that ultimately started me on the path to freedom. As my father was leaning over, talking to me, and my brother was mowing the lawn, in the blink of an eye, my father collapsed at my feet. Later we would find out that a piece of electric wire fencing had wrapped around a mower wheel. As the blade churned through the grass at the precise moment my dad leaned over to talk to me, the blade nicked the wire, shooting it through the air until it ultimately lodged in my father's neck, piercing his spinal cord. He immediately fell to the ground, unconscious and motionless, while I screamed for my mother inside the house. By the time she reached us, my father had regained consciousness but was still motionless and confused. Even in that dire moment, my mom held a question in her tone as she asked him if she should call 911 and he still hesitated—fearful of the bill.

He asked me if he was bleeding and I told him I couldn't see any blood, but then I spotted it, trickling out of his neck. Once we saw that, my parents decided to call 911. As we waited for the ambulance his body became racked with pain. We later found out the extreme pain was the nerve endings going haywire, but at the time all he could say was that it felt like he was on fire. And as he lay there waiting for help to arrive, with us hovering over him, it began to rain. He was crying out in pain; the raindrops felt like knives stabbing him all over.

The ambulance rushed my father to the local hospital, and I'll never forget the helplessness and despair as all five of us kids sat in that waiting room, hearing his agonizing screams. For a while the doctors thought he was having a mental breakdown and wanted to admit him to the psych ward. But they finally did a CT scan and found the wire still lodged in his neck and saw the hole in his spinal cord. They then transferred him to a larger hospital about an hour away where he was told he would never walk again.

Our lives changed forever.

When my dad became paralyzed, several people from our religious circle came to visit him in the hospital. Some came with flowers and kind words. But plenty of others didn't come to hold my father's hand while he and my family worked through this new reality.

No.

What several church members came to tell him as he lay in a hospital bed was that everything happening to him was a consequence of some secret sin, and he needed to confess it to be forgiven.

That rejection from the church didn't just shake him; it shook me. Then, about nine years after that tragic freak accident, my family faced the ultimate rejection: excommunication from the church. My father had questioned the pastor's son's behavior regarding the church's finances. (The concern eventually proved to be true and the pastor's son was arrested, charged with, and convicted of embezzling.)

The church—that cult—wasn't who they claimed they were. The things I had seen other families be excommunicated over were now being used to excommunicate my own family. The people who had been our chosen family for seventeen years turned their backs on us in the blink of an eye—to protect their own interests.

Every other time families had been excommunicated, the church had explained it to us in a way that made sense. They made the family who had to leave appear dishonest. They justified it. And sometimes the reason seemed valid—like when someone in leadership had molested a youth. But other times . . . other times we were just told to trust the church. They knew everything. They knew better.

When it happened to my family, I couldn't buy it. Till then I still very much followed their rules—even later, as a twenty-one-year-old living halfway across the country, if I broke a rule, even without them seeing, I was racked by guilt. If I listened to forbidden contemporary Christian music, I would feel ashamed. I still even followed their dress code for the most part, especially considering how traumatizing it was to see my mother's reaction if I didn't (like the one time I came home from college and couldn't find my pajama shorts or several other pieces of clothing in my suitcase, only to find out my mother had taken them outside and burned them).

I lived in constant fear of disappointing the church, my parents, and God.

But then the church blowup happened over my father, and something in my brain switched. I may not have been able to see how clearly wrong the church had been regarding me, but I certainly could see the facts about my parents: I had spent my life watching them pour their lives into the church. They had sacrificed *everything* the pastor told them to without question for seventeen years. They struggled. They gave when they had nothing to give. There was no valid reason to force them and my brothers out of the church. This had to be about something else . . .

And for the first time, I saw behind the curtain.

The excommunication of my parents opened my mind to new perceptions and questions. If this was how the people I got all my beliefs from acted, could I believe anything the pastor—or the church—had ever preached?

It's no surprise that I wandered for nearly a decade after I left the church. And I can admit that for a long time I had no moral compass. After breaking away from my church and the hundreds of rules and regulations, the choices were overwhelming. Suddenly I found myself thinking several times a day, *So if they were wrong and I can wear shorts, what can't I wear? If they were wrong and I can watch a movie, what can't I watch? If they were wrong about drinking, how much is too much?*

What was truth? What was healthy? What was wrong and what was good? With hundreds of boundary lines scrubbed away, I was suddenly living in a world with no bounds. In my twenties I had to paint those boundaries from scratch. I had to figure out what I believed. I had to learn how to think for myself. (More on that in the next chapter.)

What I came to realize is that God does not see me, a woman, as a second-rate human. No, God loved me and formed me in the womb to be *exactly* what I was meant to be. A woman. Just as intelligent.

Just as loved. Free to have dreams outside the ones men in some building handpicked for me.

So when it came time to build our farmhouse, to sit down with men, to discuss framing packages or windows, I didn't shy away. When the men in the industry kept directing their questions toward my husband instead of me, when men dropped by to lend a hand while I was building walls with my bare hands, I didn't feel ashamed offering up advice from the knowledge I'd gained through experience. Even when comment after comment came—and still comes—on social media by misogynistic men belittling me and telling me to stop pretending I did anything more than hold the camera while my husband did all the work, I don't let them get to me.

Because I know what it's like to live under a man's thumb in a man's world, and I know that's not God's intention. I know that's not what God made me to be.

I am a woman.

And I am strong.

Pressing On

There were plenty of discouraging moments in our build, but the lowest point, the time when I felt most discouraged, was in the beginning, right after the foundation was put in place. We were out there putting in the flooring system, which is before the framing of walls but after the foundation and stem walls. Daniel and I were out there, just the two of us, working ten-to-twelve-hour days, and I would look back and see that we had finished a total of five feet. And I would just be like, "How in the world are we *ever* going to get this done?" It just felt so impossible. So overwhelming.

I came to the harsh reality that it wasn't going to take days, but *months* just to put in this flooring system. Not to mention the work it was going to take to do the rest of the house, just the two of us. I felt like the house was never, ever, *ever* going to get done.

By trade, my husband typically worked on the final flooring and didn't have experience with framing flooring systems, and he was afraid to let anybody else come in and help—not just because we were tight on funds, but because he thought that we had to get the flooring system *flawless*. At this point Daniel had been doing flooring, which is considered a "finish" in the home-building process, for fifteen years. He had painfully dealt with out-of-square rooms and uneven flooring systems so many times that he wanted our flooring system and framing to be *perfect* so our floors would go in easier. Like, over-the-top, meticulously perfect. He did not realize that in framing, it's okay to be off a bit because it's about efficiency, not perfection.

And that's where our ignorance about some of the tasks during the build made our job even harder. There were times we just didn't know what we could get away with or what was standard. He didn't know, for example, that in the framing world, there's some give-and-take. It's okay when floors aren't absolutely level to within a centimeter. The rest of the build doesn't rely on that centimeter or go bust.

But we didn't know that. So there we were, out there with the level, and Daniel would check it and fix it and check it again and fix it again, and then checking that one would knock the other one off and he'd go back and fix that one, and on and on and on we'd go. By dinnertime we'd look back and see we'd accomplished almost nothing.

And that was so discouraging.

It was so easy in that moment to think, *What have I gotten myself into? We don't have the know-how to do this. We spent an extreme amount of money jumping into this dream, and we're dead.*

I had learned from the experiences of my childhood to press on even when the going got rough.

But we pressed on.

Neither Daniel nor I threw in the towel on those harsh days or in the months that followed. Part of the reason was that I had learned from the experiences of my childhood to press on even when the going got rough.

I could give in and say, *Forget it. This is just too embarrassing. People think we're crazy dreamers for this anyway. We'll just find another rental since our landlords want to sell where we are now and give up on this nonsense.* But I didn't let those around me affect my decisions when they thought I was foolish for leaving the church, and look how well it turned out for me. I could've given up then and silently gone back into the church, pulling on my culottes and quietly waiting for my turn to be courted by a man, but I didn't, and look at the precious man by my side now. My life now. My freedom now.

None of that came easy. I had to hack my way, often blindly, through the weeds every step of the way. Not able to tangibly see my goal in the distance but knowing it was there, and I just had to keep going. And now here I am.

So I made the decision to keep pressing on in the house build. And our work was soon rewarded.

Chapter 3

FINDING RELIEF
IN THE MIDST OF
DISCOURAGEMENT

Once we had a verbal agreement on our land, it was time to secure financing, and we set our sights on a USDA loan. Where we were planning to build was considered rural, so I did a ton of research and could find only one bank that offered a construction-to-permanent USDA loan—a company located somewhere in the Midwest.

So we emailed them, sending our plans and documentation, and for six months they basically toyed with us. They responded on occasion but mostly let us dangle. And so we waited, until finally they came back and said, "Unfortunately, this is just too big of a house for us. We don't feel comfortable financing a home this size." Given that we had provided the plans *the day* we applied and the bank knew the *exact* square footage from moment one, the rejection email only compounded our frustration.

The owners of the land had given us a year to secure financing to buy the land from them, so it was stressful losing six months just like that. The bank's news put us in hyperspeed trying to find a loan that would fit our needs, and eventually a local bank pulled through. But the contract with the land's owners expired during this process, and we ended up going over the allotted time.

The owners were incredibly gracious, however, refusing to pull out of our deal even when bigger, better cash offers came forward—some even double the price we were planning to pay. But no. They surprised us not only by refusing to hear out those offers but by extending our contract to give us another year as well. In good ol' rural Florida style, those precious people were like, "No. We're going to hold it for them. We gave them our word, and we don't back down from our word."

And as touched as I was by their kindness, the whole experience was still stressful, still disheartening. Not only had we waited seven years just to find the land, the struggle to come up with a loan and to get all the financing sorted out took much longer than we antici- pated. We had been dreaming of building our home for so long but had no clue what all we would have to go through. And we hadn't even started *building* at that point!

But I was no stranger to low seasons. I was no stranger to pressing on no matter how I felt in the moment—despite when dis- couragement, even depression, nagged. And if I could press through my past, through situations much harsher than what I was facing now, I could certainly do this too.

I was ten when my father bought us a puppy. He was beautiful. A petite chocolate Labrador who chewed at your toes and licked your face until you laughed. We named him Bear.

I was obsessed, as I was with all little animals back then.

Then, a couple days later, I came home to discover my dad had shot him.

I don't remember why my father shot him, possibly something to do with chickens. But ultimately it boiled down to this: in a mentally unstable moment he decided he didn't want the puppy anymore, and like many other times in my childhood—such as when the new television came one day and had a hole in the screen the next or the times he lashed out in anger at us kids, a switch or belt in hand—he decided to take action, believing he was given permission, even com- manded by God, to violently act.

That kind of behavior was normal for me growing up. Not only because my father struggled with depression but because of the radical institution that excused any violent behavior done by the patriarch. They took the ancient verse about "sparing the rod, spoiling the child" to heart, to the point that even a child was once killed at the hand of his father during a time of punishment, and other fathers within our same religious circles not only excused it but took it as God's divine will.

Yes, it upset me to lose my puppy, but I was so used to my dad's mood swings and such religious rationale that him shooting the dog wasn't that shocking. It was typical life. Wasn't this everyone else's reality behind closed doors? A roller coaster all the time?

My great-grandmother Mary was severely depressed, emphasized by the fact that her husband was a raging, abusive alcoholic. This played a hand in why she beat her kids. One day she was trying to beat her son for some misbehavior. He ran away, jumped a fence, fell, and broke his hip. As punishment, Mary didn't take him to the doctor. For the rest of his life, he walked with a limp. My grandmother, too, faced severe depression and mood swings and was on Prozac most of her life. Then, as I've said, my dad struggled with it.

So it wasn't entirely surprising that at an early age I started to show signs of depression too. At the age of twelve the depression was so bad I tried to take my own life.

There were so many factors: my father was dealing with a life-changing injury, and my mother was consumed with caring for him; we kids were shuffled from family member to family member, no sense of normalcy whatsoever; our family was facing the financial stress of my father being out of work and the mounting medical bills.

I had no friends; my only friend had moved away. I was stuck in this small, extremist community, either at home or at a harsh, lonely school, surrounded by nothing but chaos. Even at twelve, I remember feeling like I couldn't live that way anymore. So on one particularly bad day, I decided I was going to do it—the thing I had thought about so many times before but had never had the guts to try—I was going to kill myself.

I opened the medicine cabinet and picked out the first bottle I could find. Something I knew you weren't supposed to eat a lot of. I chewed up the entire bottle of cherry-flavored children's Tylenol and went to sleep, hoping that would be the end of me. That I wouldn't have to wake up to the insanity anymore.

Of course, since I'm telling you this story today, you know that didn't work. I woke up, surprisingly without any ill effects. I lived through that harsh season of life, and while I wouldn't say I necessarily learned my biggest lessons then, it did help prepare me to overcome when I was hit hard again about a decade later.

When my family was excommunicated from the church, we thought we had lost everything. That is how cults work. They trap you in and make you think that if you ever get out, you're doomed. And while leaving may seem like no big deal, or even worth celebrating— *Yay! You guys got out of that place; why aren't you ecstatic?*—the reality is that for my family, despite the church itself being broken and controlling and manipulative and *completely* wrong in so many ways, this group was our life.

And my parents, who were wrongfully shamed and kicked to the curb solely because my father observed missing funds and tried to point it out, were devastated. My dad didn't just lose his job within the church—my parents' main source of income. They also had no savings. No relationships outside the church. No real links with the outside world. They were completely crushed.

My younger brothers were even expelled from the church school, which had served as their meager but only social circle.

It all hit the fan. And it hit the fan hard.

I was in Florida, going to Bible college, working hard, and knowing that my family was falling apart. My father was deeply depressed, my mom traumatized, and my brothers miserable—all while my hands were tied. That moment made me question everything. *Everything.*

The pastor was a sham. The church was broken. They'd lied. Everything they'd said must be a lie too. So . . . why can't I drink? Why can't I go out to a club?

And all too soon, I found the answers.

Alcohol had never touched my lips before that moment. But the second I discovered it, I went off the deep end and hung out there for six months. Partying, going to clubs. You wouldn't expect such simple activities to dramatically change someone's life, but let me tell you: for me it changed *everything.*

I met Josh during that time. He was six feet five. He was charming. He was the life of the party. Three months after we met, three months into that new, exciting life so foreign to anything I'd ever experienced, I found out I was pregnant.

And everything I'd had going was suddenly . . . gone. All my plans, my hard work—gone.

We dashed down to the courthouse. I sealed myself in marriage to a man I hardly knew. Sealed myself to a man who would turn out, as I discovered soon enough, to be the opposite of what I had expected.

My world was completely flipped upside down—all because of a few bad decisions. All because of a few nights trying out a different life. All that immediate change again triggered that deep, dark depression that would take me to the ledge.

We lost the baby.

And on top of that grief, I was suddenly stuck in a marriage I'd never wanted.

Then Josh's own issues starting spiraling out of control, and I felt worse than stuck. I needed something better than children's Tylenol. I needed to make this better or I was going to drown.

Cornered, I zoned in on the one thing I thought could fix everything: having a baby. I had lost the one, so maybe, just maybe, if I had another one, that would make everything better. Maybe that would heal the hole inside me, fix him, fix our marriage, and make our lives work. Obviously I'd screwed up my old life plans at Bible college. I might as well make new ones.

And I did get pregnant again. But even after I had my daughter, I was still depressed. In fact, I loathed myself. I loathed my life. I succumbed to an eating disorder and let the number on the scale dictate my happiness.

Then things with my husband began to get really bad. He was out of control and eventually did things that I just couldn't ignore anymore.

I moved out.

And oh, wasn't it all so painful. The grief of living a life I never wanted. The depression I masked so well. All compounded by the guilt that I was now separated from my husband when, in my family, *nobody* got a divorce. No one knew how low I felt.

Getting a divorce was the one thing in the world that *nobody* did. Abuse your kids? Manipulate them? Withhold love? Fine. But divorce? *Never. That* was the sin that mattered. That was the sin I could never overcome.

And then I got pregnant again, with the husband I'd just separated from. Whatever you're thinking now, I've heard it. Not only did I carry criticism from those who didn't support my decision to move out, I also gained new criticism the moment I saw those two faint pink lines on the pregnancy strip. How could I have gone back to him, even momentarily? What was I thinking? I'd almost gotten out. I was almost *free*.

Then suddenly there I was, alone, pregnant with my second child.

Broken.

But in that moment of being pushed so deep into that dark hole, of really hitting rock bottom, I found a pebble of strength. In that moment of feeling *so bad*, I realized I had to do something, right then, or I was going to die.

That's when I *finally* went to a doctor, got counseling, and began to work through my issues. My exterior problems didn't end there, but it was a powerful moment and the mark of a fresh beginning.

Eventually, out of nothing but pure desperation, I turned to the Bible. Because I had to do something to stop the voice inside my head that was hounding me day after day, telling me, *You're now a single mother because of your failure to stay in the church . . . just like they said would happen. Your life no longer has value. Your mistakes are all you are. Everything they said would happen without them has happened.* And in a desperate attempt to salvage my ruined life, I turned to the only thing I knew: my religion. But this time, in reading the Bible, I discovered a way so radically different from anything I had ever been taught.

Instead of merely listening to what the pastor told me, I read and realized that the Bible was *much* more than fire and brimstone and rules and regulations; it was about a relationship with a Being who *wanted* to know me and loved me, failures and all.

Years later, when I spent hours hovering over my computer, scurrying around trying to find a good option for a loan, all the while knowing the clock was ticking and that at any moment our dream

The Bible was <u>much</u> more
than fire and brimstone
and rules and regulations;
it was about a relationship
with a Being who <u>wanted</u>
to know me and loved
me, failures and all.

land could be snatched from us, I leaned on the lessons learned through counseling and my own Scripture reading and didn't let my discouragement win. I set my chin and kept on, even when I felt like crying out in frustration, because I'd learned that I had the option to let my emotions win or my determination.

And that day, like many more to come throughout the build, I let my determination win.

Chapter 4

LEARN ON THE JOB

Shortly before my divorce, I met a girl who was hosting a Bible study in her home. After the dust of my divorce had settled, she invited me to her home for a barbecue where, unbeknownst to me, she had also invited her friend Daniel, hoping that at best sparks might fly and at worst two of her good friends could also become friends. Well, let's just say there was a fireworks show that night. A week later we had our first date, and from that moment on we were inseparable. Eight months later, Daniel proposed.

During this time, I was living in a townhome and Daniel was renting a room at his uncle's house. As we made plans for what our lives would look like once we got married, we talked about how much money we were throwing away each month and what our long-term goals were. I was working in banking but ultimately wanted to be a stay-at-home mom. Daniel wanted to grow his tile and flooring business enough that he wasn't just working *in* it but *over* it.

And of course, there was Daniel's lifelong dream to build his own home.

The question was, How were we going to do it all? We wanted to set ourselves up for success but certainly didn't have the finances or freedom to do so with the way we were living.

So we asked ourselves, Do we really want to rent a tiny condo for $1,800 a month in this expensive area where we live so our kids can stare at the wall all day? Do we really want to go without a yard? Do we want to stretch our finances to the max simply paying for our condo and cars?

We sat down with Daniel's business-savvy parents, had a

drawn-out conversation about our options, and decided to make the jump. And truly, it was a *jump* into a no-holding-back commitment to cutting serious things out of our life to make room for our dreams.

We sold both of our cars.

We got an old, old, *old* Suburban so Daniel could get to work each day.

I stayed home with my two daughters. No car. Just me. And them. At home. All the time.

Then another drastic money-saving opportunity came: leave our rental and buy a camper from a family friend. They let us finance it for $300 a month. For two years we lived in that camper: Daniel, me, and our two girls. Two years of making meals in that tiny kitchen quite literally as big as one step in either direction. Two years of showering in bathrooms as big as refrigerator cardboard boxes. Two years.

But you know what happened at the end of those two years? What came from the fruit of that labor? At the end we not only owned the camper outright but were able to sell it and get the *same amount* back. So we essentially came out not only having had free lodging for two years but we were also able to save all that money we would've spent renting a condo.

It was a major win because instead of throwing our money away on rent, we put every penny we had into the business. Building it. Fanning the flame so that when the opportunity came to jump into building our own farmhouse, we were financially *and* emotionally ready to get creative for the sake of our dreams.

And sure enough, we had to get creative from the get-go.

Initially we had intended to get only the shell of the house in place and take our time finishing it as funds appeared. The goal was to get in and then do DIY projects over the next five years to finish it out. We never planned on doing anything custom. We never expected high-end. We were just shooting for the minimum requirements to get our certificate of occupancy. One working bathroom. Water. Just the bare bones.

But at the very first hoop in the process, our game plan changed.

We went to lunch with a lumber rep and window installer just a couple of months after closing on the loan. During the conversation they mentioned something about a system called Ready-Frame. The instant one of them mentioned it, the other gave him a look that screamed, "What are you doing? *Hush.*" Following a couple of seconds of awkward silence, the rep tried to move on.

That's when I spoke up, asking for clarification.

Turns out, Ready-Frame is a system like an old Sears home kit. Your house comes precut and labeled in packages and you put it together like one giant puzzle. The company optimizes the house plan in their computer system so that you get the most efficient cut of each piece of wood, meaning minimal waste on the jobsite instead of losing dumpsters' worth of cut wood. They explained that on a difficulty scale of 0 to 10, this was probably a 3, maybe a 4. They said that our teenage daughter could even help if she wanted.

And the biggest appeal? It was $40,000 cheaper than hiring a framer.

At that point our goal wasn't to DIY every single aspect of the house. We had planned on doing some of it ourselves, but we certainly hadn't planned on getting so deep into the work that we would be *framing.* Tiling, sure. That was Daniel's specialty. But framing? That was serious stuff.

But there we were, not even into the dig of our new build, and suddenly aware of this truly out-of-the-box opportunity. We knew we had to do it. How could we not? If we could do this job ourselves, we could save $40,000.

So Daniel went out with a friend, and together they dug the footers and built the stem-walls. They got everything ready.

Then we began framing the walls.

And I'll never forget seeing the eighteen-wheeler driving down our little one-lane road. The massive flatbed with piles of lumber reaching toward the sky, the word *JETT* stamped on each piece of wood. I'll never forget how Daniel and I looked at each other, mutually in awe of our decision, the thought running through both our minds, *What on earth are we doing? What have we gotten ourselves into?*

The drivers pulled up and dumped the lumber onto our property. Then the rep hopped out and said, "All right, guys. You ready to build a house?"

And while we stood there *completely* overwhelmed, he handed us a guidebook about six inches thick. Every page full of foreign words about studs, jacks, kings, nothing on the page making sense.

Mind you, this was directly after Daniel and I had undertaken the flooring system. This was after I had spent days out there with him, all but pulling my hair out while he tracked *every little* piece of wood we touched with a level, out there for ten hours and making five feet of progress. I thought we were going to spend the rest of our lives doing that stupid flooring system . . . but this?

Throw in giant pieces of lumber that *we* somehow were supposed to pull together, all by ourselves, like ants trying to piece together a castle. Having no clue what we were doing.

It was insane.

Suffice it to say, I was freaking out. There were only *two* of us. *Two* of us to do all this work, with four children and another business to manage all day long.

It was impossible.

Right?

Smiling—no doubt a little forced—I asked the rep, "So, where do we start?" And basically he shrugged and said, "Wherever you want. Just pick a wall and go."

So, that's what we did.

We picked the front of the house, held close that little manual, and started building walls. We'd look at the guide for whatever wall we wanted to put up, study the diagram showing where the top plate and bottom plate were located, count all the X's signifying all the studs we'd need, get them from the pile, and put them together.

Even with occasional help from a friend, it was still exhausting and labor-intensive and, honestly, frequently mind-boggling. The house was *so big.* We didn't just start this with a tiny square of a home. It was tall. It was complicated. It was enormous. So many times I'd have to step back and think, *Is this really happening? Can this really get done?*

But sure enough, by our third wall, I finally was like, "Okay. We got this. We can do this."

Unlike those plots of land you drive by that are empty one day and framed in the next, it was at least three months until we were finally dried in. It was not a quick process. It was not a simple process. It was certainly not a lazy process. But we did it. It certainly would've been easier if we'd had the funds to hire somebody to do it, or if we were master builders ourselves, with years of education and experience under our belts. But the reality was we really could, quite literally, build our own home from the ground up without experience. We just needed to dive in.

Neither Daniel nor I have a college degree, but we not only built a 3,700-square-foot home with no experience but also grew a social media following to more than 4 million followers while landing over $1 million in brand deals.

We tried out these dreams with no experience. And yet here we are. Learning to be proud of those facts about ourselves. Learning to value the willingness to strategically learn new things more than anything that could've been taught to us fifteen years ago in a textbook.

But for a long time, I let the fact that I never finished college weigh me down. I thought I needed to go back and finish up my degree if I really wanted to make something of my life. I felt like a dropout, doomed to never succeed beyond a certain point. And that bothered me.

To my parents, there were two major definers of success: One, to be someone in the ministry. Two, to have successfully completed your college degree in ministry. The perfect concoction? To somehow combine the two.

But there I was, the only one in the family not only to have gotten pregnant "out of wedlock" but to have dropped out of school *just* before graduation—all the while having two brothers in ministry and with advanced degrees.

Noell, the black sheep.

Noell, the failure.

So every few months for a long time, I'd research classes. Over the years I'd throw out the question while raising my kids and working my day job, "Is now a good time to go back? What if I commuted? What about this or that online class?"

The idea was always in the back of my mind as the thing to do when the time came.

For years I'd have nightmares as well. Of not finishing . . . again. Of getting up to the point of taking the diploma and missing it. Of getting calls from the secretary of my high school saying she just discovered I had never graduated high school either and had to hurry back. I'd even have the opposite dream, where I'd get my college degree and feel so great, only to wake up and realize it was not reality.

I had the hanging fear that I had set up myself, my life, for failure. All because I was missing that prized piece of paper.

Then I met Daniel.

And his reaction to my fears was so simple, so immediate. *You don't need a college degree, Noell. What are you talking about?* After he assured me of that enough times, after I sat back and took a good look at the thriving life our family already had, I started, inch by inch, to loosen my grip on that faulty belief. I started to realize the lie I had been fed by our culture for what it was.

And not so surprisingly, the nightmares stopped.

That realization years ago lent a hand to why we were so willing to try to build a house ourselves.

To us, success doesn't mean having a college degree; it means having financial stability, doing what we're passionate about, and having freedom with our time. Every year we make it a goal to have six one-week vacations with our family. The vacation doesn't have to be to an extravagant location; it's not about big flights to tropical islands. We want to take time with our family to explore, to disconnect from the outside world, and to lean into each other. Having sources of income that allow for those vacations is a major factor in our definition of success.

Of course, some jobs require degrees—we certainly wouldn't expect anyone to perform brain surgery without that row of documentation proving they were experts in their field—but *many* vibrant careers these days do not require degrees.

Look at Bill Gates. Or Jessica Alba. Or Ralph Lauren. Or Jan Koum. Or Ty Warner. Or Beyoncé. Or even Prince Harry.

Perhaps the most famous and worthy example of this is Mark Zuckerberg. After creating the social media platform known as Facebook in his Harvard dorm room, he dropped out of college. Can you imagine what a leap that was for him? To see a spark he had created start to glow and to drop the traditional career path, the safe route, to pour his energies into fanning the flame? It's no surprise that twelve years later Harvard awarded him an honorary degree while he delivered the commencement speech. But that's the rub: he didn't *need* that piece of paper announcing he could proceed on the road to success. He was *already* the most successful person in the room.

Did you know that one in eight billionaires on the 2018 ranking of the Forbes 400 wealthiest people in America was a college dropout? But perhaps you are thinking, *That's all fine and good for geniuses, actresses, and princes, but for the average Joe you have to stay on course to get anywhere.*

Well, in that case, look at us. I don't have a master's degree in marketing from a prestigious college. Daniel isn't a licensed general contractor working with a nationally recognized building company. But if we could have any life in the world, we would pick ours.

My heart breaks for friends of mine who, fifteen years after college, are still paying heavily for tuition costs of a degree they didn't end up needing. They have loans they will be paying on for the rest of their lives. And maybe they could have avoided it if they'd simply stopped and asked themselves: *Are we just following the crowd, or do we actually need this to do what we want?*

So, before you choose a certain path in life, be sure to ask yourself, *Is there a way to work around the system?*

Daniel is living out his dream running a small business. After high school he started working on his associate degree. But to sum it up, he hated it. He hated taking the tests. He hated being stuck in class, learning about topics he was never going to use. Spending money to be sitting in a chair when he could be out there working with his hands, really learning.

College just wasn't for him.

But his dream was to be an entrepreneur. His dad had always taught him how important it was to grow his own business. He knew that's what he wanted to do; he just didn't quite know how to put his goals into practice.

Consequently, at age twenty-two he connected with a skilled flooring and tile contractor and became his apprentice. And as real-life experience—as opposed to reading about it in a textbook—is a much quicker indicator of how you'll actually like the job, Daniel realized early on that this was the field for him. He enjoyed producing things. He enjoyed the art of building. And with that direction in mind, he narrowed down the field he would pursue.

Relationships Are Everything

Through twelve years in banking before all this farmhouse stuff began, I learned that to be successful in *anything*, truly just about *anything*, you have to put yourself out there and be likable. I say that not to mean you should be inauthentic or play on the emotions of others for your own personal gain. No, I simply mean you need to think, *What kind of person would I want to talk to in this moment?*

Would I want to talk to someone who is authoritative but also overbearing, arrogant, and rude? Or someone who listens to others, engages with them in conversation, and shows respect at all times? Obviously the latter.

Learn to ask open-ended questions. Learn how to overcome objections. Be genuine. Care.

While yes, I certainly could've learned these tactics and methods while in a classroom studying marketing and advertising, I learned them through life experience just as well. And those life skills were a major reason I was able to turn @jettsetfarmhouse into a success.

In fact, the book you are holding in your hands or listening to at this very moment is a perfect example of how being available and attentive to others can lead to golden opportunities. In response to one of my Instagram posts, a girl commented, and fairly soon it became apparent she was a writer within the publishing house of my dreams. She was intrigued by the story of how our family had built our farmhouse with our own hands, and by the end of the day she was telling me she'd be happy to pitch my story to her team. The next day she called her editor. That editor liked our story and talked to another editor. And within twelve hours I got an email from the publisher asking if I wanted to pursue a book. That random girl chatting with me on Instagram ended up not only hearing and encouraging me in my story but helping me get a two-book deal and sign with a top literary agent—and she even became my cowriter on this very book.

(Side note: I say all this while needing to clarify something. There's a fine line between showing the likable part of yourself and manipulating others, and I want to make clear that the *last* thing I would ever want to do, or ever recommend anyone else do, is be inauthentic to fit whatever mold you think people want. I never pretended to be somebody else to grow my social media account. I just knew the basics: people want people who share stories, and they don't want to be preached at. People want to connect with others, not feel spammed. So please don't pretend to raise a thousand animals on your nonexistent farm if that's not who you are. Don't dye

Learn to ask
open-ended questions.
Learn how to
overcome objections.
Be genuine. Care.

your hair and buy new clothes to fit an edgy bookish aesthetic if it isn't genuine. Be you. The world needs *you*. The social media platform is a *huge* platform, and there truly is room for everybody to find their people. The most important thing you need to do is be willing to share. The number-one thing people *don't* connect with is people who hold their cards high, unwilling to share a shred of detail about their personal lives all the while expecting everyone to follow them.)

The other things I needed to learn to succeed on social media I was willing to learn as I went. It didn't take long to learn that on social media I only had one to three seconds to make a connection before people would decide whether to scroll on or not. I learned by trying things out that I had an extremely short amount of time to evoke an emotion that would draw people toward me in a real and authentic way. And I knew from both life experience and diving into the app that I needed to be mindful to express *who* I am and *what* I'm about as quickly as possible.

And sure enough, it worked. My account started growing, quite rapidly in fact, because I shared about my life and passions in a way that people in my niche felt they could connect with. And best of all, I learned these things *on the job*, instead of doing something like signing up for online courses.

So please don't undervalue your life experiences. In many careers there are opportunities to learn as you go. And if you already have a clear goal in mind, what's stopping you?

Chapter 5

INSTAGRAM: WHERE IT ALL BEGAN

A month before we closed on the loan for the new build, I had started an Instagram account. We were still in a rental house, before the camper. We had received the okay for clearing the land and were working round the clock. One evening Daniel and I were sitting on the carpeted home office of our rental, trying to get the budget filled out for the bank's approval, and we had a question about one part of the material. So we went online to where we got our floor plan, ArchitecturalDesigns.com, and while looking at our plan we were surprised to see a new feature on the page: a client album. We said, "Oh, that's so cool. You can see everything from someone's house." And while we were looking through a slew of their beautiful photos, we saw a space that said, more or less, "You can also see this build at such-and-such handle on Instagram."

Until that point I had thought of Instagram as just a place to add filters for my personal photos. You know: add the little Nashville filter to a photo of my children to then put on Facebook. That kind of thing.

Given this new information, however, I searched that girl's Instagram handle and discovered she had over twenty thousand followers. *Twenty thousand.* And all she'd ever done was share construction pictures of the house built from the same plan that we were about to use.

So I reached out to her via direct message saying, "Hi. We're getting ready to build the same house you have, and I was wondering if you have any advice or would do anything differently." And super sweetly, she wrote me back.

It wasn't a lightning-strike conversation where inspiration immediately sparked, but it was enough for me to step away with a thought: *Hold on here. If this girl can have* twenty thousand followers *by sharing construction pictures, then maybe I could get followers too. If she could get that kind of following from other people building her house, then maybe we'd have an extra unique hook because we're primarily doing this ourselves.*

So I started, with the original dream of getting five thousand followers and perhaps finding some way to use the account to sell home goods or something similar in the future. But there was another reason I started using Instagram. Part of it had to do with taking time for myself. I wanted to start an account for *me*. I wanted a creative outlet to give me a break from the chaos I was dealing with the other twenty-three hours of the day.

You see, my husband was, and has always been, way better at taking time for himself than me. Maybe it's because men typically have an easier time compartmentalizing and setting aside the stress of life and family to pursue whatever they want to do in that moment. Maybe it's because I cannot *not* think about the calendar running constantly in my head—how this kid has to go to that and this kid has to be picked up from here and we have all these things to manage and . . .

It was and is endless. My brain just can't shut off.

At the time, my youngest, Crew, was two. And for those two years since his birth, he was draining. Like, *draining.*

When he was five days old and we were at the pediatrician's office, Crew unrelentingly held his breath and screamed. Finally the pediatrician looked at me and said, "You have a stubborn one on your hands, don't you?" Then Crew promptly peed on both of us.

At that moment I knew he was going to be a handful. And he

was. He'd hold his breath and pass out if he didn't get his way. When frustrated or scared or angry or hungry or anything *at all* besides perfectly happy, he would scream. For hours on end. Anytime we got in the car, he'd scream. Three hours later, still screaming.

One day as I was dropping my daughter off for homeschool co-op, I realized I was going to be driving three hours a day, three days a week, for a year with my handsome, adorable, beloved infant son—who was also my indefatigable siren. For twelve hours a week I was going to hear his screeching wails behind my head. Pounding in my ears. Sapping my will to live. And for those first years of his life, I made a mistake and did something I shouldn't have done: I stayed home and did nothing but parent.

All the time.

We hired someone to work with Daniel in the company, replacing me, and all I did, day and night, was parent. Change diapers. Keep the kids from falling into moving vehicles or grabbing knives. Feed them. Clean them up. Wake up and do it all again.

It felt too hard to get out and take time for myself, so I didn't.

I fell into this mom slump, and for a while I thought I'd never get out of it.

One day I passed a gym and thought, *I don't even remember what it's like to go inside a gym. In fact, I don't even remember what it's like to have the* desire *to get up and get dressed to go there.*

I was losing my identity. It got to the point where I was like, "I have to do something for myself that I want to do, without any motherly motive, or I'm going to go crazy."

And so, when the thought surfaced of starting to utilize Instagram, both for myself and as a potential way to make money and build a brand one day, I was ecstatic. Instagram as a form of entertainment and a creative outlet was cheap. Cheap and portable and easy to do anywhere, anytime. A way to take a mental break for myself but also potentially earn out in the end. It was a win-win scenario.

And sure enough, it gave me community; it gave me a sense of purpose; it gave me an entertaining outlet where I learned more about things I was interested in. For me, it was exactly what I needed.

I'm still pretty bad at taking time for myself. I run the business hard, I run the household hard, and frankly, I find it hard to stop because, well, how do you just stop when you're in the middle of spinning so many plates? How do you stop without breaking one?

But I'm learning.

And preaching to myself as much as to you, here's what I learned as both a hardworking mother and an entrepreneur.

Get Rid of That Mom Guilt and Do What You Love

Mom shaming is real.

We see it and we feel it, over every little decision in our family's lives. And we know it's truly over *everything*.

How many kids do you put in one bedroom? Isn't four a little much? You know, I was just reading an article on a study contrasting kids who had their own private "safe space" versus those jammed into one room like pigs . . .

Oh, your kids *all* have their own bedrooms? Wow. Yeah no, our family prioritizes minimalism over the American addiction to clutter.

Your kids stay up *that* late?

Your kids go to bed *how* early?

You put them in *those* swimming lessons? Don't you know they basically waterboard them?

You put them in *those* swimming lessons? Don't you know the floaties they use will basically train them to drown when you aren't looking?

Of course we vaccinated them. We aren't psychos.

Of course we didn't vaccinate them. We aren't psychos.

And one thing it's so easy to do as moms is fear we are going to be judged for spending any time on ourselves.

It is so easy to look at that mom who runs around like the Energizer Bunny, never taking an ounce of time for herself, and feel like you're a failure. After all, Joanne bounces around baking energizer balls while pregnant with her fourth kid and working as an esteemed orthodontist on the side. Her sweet potato casseroles are perfect. She never complains or, apparently, needs sleep. And isn't she running that marathon?

But I am not Joanne, and maybe you aren't either. I am me, you are you, and our needs are unique. Maybe Joanne truly is energized by baking. Or maybe she also is dealing with secret mom guilt and feels compelled to work that hard. Who knows? The point is, I'm learning it doesn't matter. I can just let her do her and focus on myself. "What do I need? What fills me up? What drains me?"

At the beginning of starting my Instagram, I felt bad that I wasn't completely satisfied just being Mom. I had always helped with the business and had always helped Daniel, and then when I stepped out of that position, I felt guilty for being sad. Why were there other moms who were completely fulfilled just doing the mom and wife thing and nothing else? What was wrong with me that I loved my family, absolutely, yet wanted something more?

But focusing less on analyzing others and instead turning that magnifying glass on myself freed me. Doing Instagram and having something just *for me* made me happy.

And that was, and is, a great thing.

After all, when I'm happy, my kids feel it. They sense it. My spouse senses it. And in my house, I am more responsible for the overall vibe than anyone else. So getting rid of that mom guilt built by comparison was extremely healthy for me, and if that's something you struggle with, it will be for you too.

Reach for Equality

I once saw a TikTok of a girl who said, "If our generation can achieve one thing for our society, I hope it's that men would help with the dishes too." And I was like, *"Preach, girl!"*

Because our society still expect females to do *so much*. I've seen this both throughout my childhood and, on occasion, in my life today. To give much more than our fair share and, instead of making noise about it, just quietly keep pushing on. Quietly tell ourselves, "Well, this is just the way it is" as we clean up the men's dishes after Thanksgiving while the men lounge on the couches with stuffed bellies. Quietly say, "This is just what we asked for" as we have the freedom to work, yes, but then are expected to also do most of the household chores.

In our day and age, with more dual-career marriages than not, we especially have to be mindful about protecting ourselves. This is actually a big source of stress in my marriage and, I'm guessing, many marriages.

You may relate to this picture: It's Saturday morning. We've all had a hectic week bouncing from soccer practice to doctor appointment to school and barely back in time to scrape together dinner and bath and prep to do it all again. *Finally* though, finally it's the weekend. Time to double the parenting manpower. Time to have another set of eyes supervising the situation, preparing meals, taxiing the kids around, and cleaning up the messes that seem to sprout whenever you turn around.

Time to relax.

I get up in the morning. Flip the French toast while the coffee brews. Catch the light coming through our kitchen windows. Take a breath. Smile as I hear my kids' first footsteps of the day crossing the hall. All of us. Together.

"I'm off for a few, babe." And there he stands, bright-eyed and bushy-tailed, a bag of golf clubs over his shoulder. Do you hear the lightning crackling?

Whereas he can't seem to grasp how a few hours out on a slow Saturday could possibly bother anyone, I'm about to slam my coffee cup and unleash the dragon. Whereas he hears me cry out in frustration and immediately feels like I'm trying to control him, I'm just trying to share the load.

Perhaps you've been here before.

The struggle, for me, is real.

And yet, *somehow*, I preach about this all the time to my kids. The love bank. You can't give love if your love bank is empty. You can't be your best self for others if you're dragging on your own. I talk up the power of mental health days all the time and yet struggle to follow my own rule. I, who quite frankly seem to need it the most in my family, can't relax.

Instead I, Mom, give and give and give.

All. Day. Long.

Every day running a household, every night sleeping with two babes on me. It's never-ending. And yet I know what I want and need. What fills up each person's love bank is different.

Obviously I'd love to take my paddleboard down to the intercoastal and spend every Saturday morning floating on the blue-green ocean, hearing nothing but the seagulls and my oar pushing against the tide. But when I started out, Instagram was all I needed. Maybe for you, it's going on girls' trips. Maybe your thing is dressing up for a night on the town or three-day weekends with the gals. Or perhaps it's something as simple as taking a bath after everyone's in bed.

Honestly? Even just going to the grocery store by myself sometimes does it for me. Getting out of the house, strolling the aisles, letting my imagination go about what I want to cook that week and what ingredients I'll use . . . it can truly be as simple as that.

So whatever it is—maybe getting a run in every day, going salsa dancing, reading a good book—I hope you give yourself that break too. Because we need it, don't we? We need it for our own well-being. We need it to be the best form of ourselves, which also helps us be the best form of ourselves for those around us. And there is absolutely nothing to feel guilty about.

Start Small

Even if it's just going to the grocery store by yourself, that's a start. Even if it's taking a fifteen-minute drive to Starbucks to grab a coffee in the drive-through and have a few minutes to sip in peace and quiet, that's an achievement. Little by little you can chip away at that giant block of need. Start small. Work your way up, and as you get rid of any guilt you feel as a woman or mother, as you make it okay and a norm to have that time for yourself, you can get to a point where you recognize your exact needs and have a means to fulfill them.

Everybody's needs are different. Maybe you are in a season when your days are absolutely crammed from the second the alarm goes off to the second you turn off the light at night. Maybe you are in a particularly harsh season when you have a colicky newborn and sleep deprivation is your battle. Or maybe for the most part you are doing okay and would appreciate a little reset every now and again.

Your schedule and needs may vary week by week, season by season, and with that, the amount of time you need to take for yourself will vary. So let it.

Don't just tell yourself, "I only get this one two-hour window on Thursday evenings to slip into a book because that's the way it's always been." Maybe your needs are greater that week and you really need to up the ante. Wherever you are, try to reassess your mental and emotional needs frequently so you can be your best self not just for your own sake, but for others.

Don't Undervalue Personal Hobbies

If you have poured your soul *only* into your adorable kiddos for the last two decades, you're going to struggle with your identity the moment they leave home. Who are you without your kids nearby? If they have been your *everything* and you have never pursued relationships, activities, or even thoughts outside of them, you will struggle.

My mother-in-law is a perfect example of someone who has successfully transitioned into the empty-nest season. She regularly goes to Costa Rica, Peru—truly all over the world—with her friends. They horseback ride out in jungles and taste new foods and have all these incredible adventures. And really, there was no transition into living this kind of lifestyle because she was always cautious about taking "me time." She continuously refined her hobbies and kept up with her friendships so that, yes, it was sad when her daughter left home, and yes, it was sad when her son left home, but it was far less shocking than it would've been had she not prioritized herself in addition to the children she was raising.

Wherever you are, try to reassess your mental and emotional needs frequently so you can be your best self not just for your own sake, but for others.

You don't have to go to Peru for "me time." The point is, dig inside yourself and remember those little pleasures that make you, *you*. Getting coffee with friends. Joining a dance class with friends. Just being sure to *have* friends. Whatever is a vital part of you, be sure to pencil it in just as you would your kid's soccer practice or dentist appointment or any other thing on the calendar. Because it is just as significant and worthy. It's part of keeping up being *you*.

Chapter 6

BEAUTY ON THE INSIDE

It's amazing how a person can treat you differently when you get a bit of success.

For years I had a loose friendship with someone in our community. She and her family would come over for dinners, and our children shared the same friend circle. But for some reason, I always felt a chasm between us. A wall she had put up, not noticeable to the naked eye.

But there were little clues.

The way she'd keep up a polite conversation with me only until someone else came into the room and her attention could move on to somebody else.

Or when she threw a birthday party at the lake for her daughter, but when I came to pick my daughter up after the party, I noticed all these suitcases tucked in the corner. After the fact I learned that she had welcomed every other child to stay for an extended sleepover—except for my daughter.

But then, *oh then*, my husband and I decided we were moving away from our cramped rental to a shiny, brand-new farmhouse. Then my Instagram account started to take off.

And before I knew it, I was at a group Christmas party and she was welcoming me with open arms. Chatting away wildly like we'd always been best friends. Cozying up to me all evening like there was no one else around. Wanting to talk on and on about the house. Messaging me on Instagram a week later asking for a "little favor" on a business venture she was thinking about.

I wish I could say that was the only time on this journey I

experienced going from being treated like a nobody to a somebody simply because I'd started a successful business venture and built a nicer home for my family.

But I can't.

So many people judge based on appearances. So many want to love on you not because of your character but because of how you measure up by society's standards, whether it's your body or your home or your economic status.

And as I faced both unmerited judgment—from those watching our build from the sidelines and writing us off as ostentatious for the luxury items we were so fortunate to have been given—and sudden, egregious applause from others who wouldn't so much as glance our way before our brand started taking off, I was reminded of the lesson I'd learned back in childhood: my appearance and my possessions should never define me. It's my character that counts.

My mom is five foot one, one hundred pounds dripping wet. She's been lean and slender her whole life—she and everyone else in her family. Well, everyone else except for me.

Growing up I had my fair share of curves, and slight though they may be, compared to the rest of my family, I thought I was thick. And from the time I was little, I loved to eat. I'm talking frozen then defrosted white bread we purchased at the discount baker in bulk, slathered in gravy from our Sunday pot roast. Not fancy food at unique restaurants, but cheap meals. Anything I could get my hands on. Looking back, the biggest meal of the day for us was dinner, particularly Sunday dinner. We weren't allowed to snack—the fridge was off-limits between meals—so when the opportunity

My appearance and
my possessions should
never define me.
It's my character
that counts.

came during those meals, I ate big and I ate hard. Learning to overindulge.

My dad would watch me and say, "You need to stop eating like that, Noell. You're going to be a whale someday if you keep it up."

I would also hear him tell my petite mom, "If you ever get fat, I'm going to trade you in for a skinnier model." Because that was his biggest flex for her, the thing he was most proud of: she was so tiny.

And I would hear that and think, *If he thinks she's on the verge of being considered fat, I must be a whale.* And eventually, after hearing these words so often, I began to believe them. Skinniness equals love. Food must equal fat. Therefore, to get love, I needed to avoid food.

By the time I was ten, I had developed an obsession. I would pig out on what little food we had because I love to eat, but then I would feel guilty. I would think I needed to exercise, but never did it consistently. And when I wasn't consistent, I felt even more guilt because I failed doing that as well. It was a terrible cycle of self-hatred and loathing.

It wasn't until I had a conversation with my first child, my daughter who was four at the time, that everything changed. She had just had the flu. While I was holding her, she said something to me along the lines of, "I'm so glad I got the flu, Mommy, because look how flat my tummy is." And I just remember my heart crushed in that moment. The realization of, *Oh my gosh, what am I doing? Am I saying things? Is she hearing me? Is she looking at me? Somehow she is getting this in her head that she has to be skinny.*

That's when I changed. That was the moment when I told myself, *I'm not going to do this anymore. I can't. I have to heal. I have to accept myself as is. I have to work on the things that are causing my self-hatred and dysmorphia.* Truly in that moment of hearing my four-year-old say that about her own body, I committed to changing the way I think and talk about mine.

My mindset changed.

Ever since, I have been intentional in never saying a negative word about my children's bodies or mine. All I speak is body positivity. All they ever hear from me is love and encouragement; telling them to eat all they want and need, to remember that food is here to fuel our bodies. We work out not to be skinny but because exercising makes us strong and healthy. We find clothes that fit our bodies, not the other way around. I try to build them up so that when they come face-to-face with others who try to tear them down—and in this world, they will—they will stand strong.

I like to explain to my children that no matter how unsightly a newborn may look in those first moments, a parent falls head over heels in love. When my daughter Amelia was born, half of her face was swollen and bruised, but of course I didn't think twice about it. I was in love with her. Full stop. Just as I am now.

So I ask my children, "As your mom, would you love me less if I weighed fifty pounds more? Would that weight affect how you feel about me?" No, it wouldn't. They love me no matter what.

The unfortunate thing about life is that we often judge others, and are judged ourselves, based on the wrong things.

I've lived in both poverty and wealth. As a stay-at-home mother and as a successful entrepreneur. In hand-me-downs and jean skirts that reached my toes and in pretty dresses and high heels. In forty-foot campers and in 3,700-square-foot houses. And one thing rings true: if somebody doesn't love me for who I am in one situation, they shouldn't really be in my life in the other.

So guard your heart, as I have had to guard my heart and those of my children while our accounts grew and life situations changed. Treasure those who want to come to your cookout not only when you've arranged hydrangeas on every table and have the glowing water feature trinkling merrily but also when you are in that crowded camper with barbecue sandwiches from the country gas station. Get to know the people who love you not just in your success but in your all.

Chapter 7

DUST YOURSELF OFF
AFTER REJECTION

When you grow up with the religious fanaticism I experienced, divorce—for any reason—is just about on par with murder. So being a divorced mother of two, I faced so much shame. The good little girl who had spent her life doing the right things was suddenly a single mom with two kids. I felt like I had no value. I had messed up God's plan for my life and there was no fixing it. I was "that kind of woman" now. I wore the scarlet letter.

I remember this one sermon when the pastor was shouting over the podium in his gravely southern drawl: "There ain't no bread in Moab."

Moab, in Bible times, was the equivalent of the world's sinful culture. And those who turned their chins toward Moab and traveled there, tempted by the promise of bread, were fools because there was no bread in Moab. And then, hungry and lost, they had nothing.

Well . . . I was now in Moab. In one quick, foolish move, I entered the land of loss and horror.

Come to me, men, and I'll drag you down into the darkness where I live.

And for a long time, I really had that conviction. I thought, *I am marred. I've ruined my testimony. People think I'm a horrible person.* My self-image was so bad that even when Daniel came along pursuing me, I tried to sabotage the relationship. I was so stuck in believing the lie that I was not worthy; I was too afraid to even hope that good would come.

But thankfully, Daniel's unconditional love slowly changed me. He and his family loved me from day one.

I'll never forget going over to meet his parents that first time and how terrified I was. I had played out all these scenarios in my mind about how they might react to their beloved little boy bringing home a woman like me. So much baggage. A clear troublemaker.

I cringed at the thought that they would stiffly shake my hand and then run to talk about me in hushed voices in the other room. And I was afraid they would ask me exactly what had happened for me to end up this way and how on earth I could possibly be good enough for their son.

After all, that's what I faced at home in my own family, and from anyone who heard my name in the church I grew up in. *That's who I had become.*

Right?

And yet I'll never forget that first time and how Daniel's mom smiled, so carefree, as she asked all about my two young daughters. How she cozied up beside me on the couch, eagerly wanting me to pull out my phone and show her pictures. How she enthusiastically looked forward to meeting my daughters. The actions were worth ten thousand words.

Daniel and his family slowly inserted new ideas, encouraging ideas, into my distorted worldview. And as my mind became fuller and fuller with words of encouragement and support, the lies began to slowly seep out. Little by little. Day by day. Until one day something jogged my memory about my previous mindset, and I said, "Oh yeah. I used to think that about myself. I forgot."

Making New "Friends"

But even though I am fairly healed from my past rejections, there are still moments that throw me. Three years ago, when I started this farmhouse build on our social media, I had no idea what was going to come of it. Never for a moment did I think to myself, *Yes, this is a place where I am eventually going to share my story and be a role model—not just about farmhouse design but about life.* Even when companies started reaching out to me for brand deals, I had no thought or consideration for what this would eventually lead to.

And yet as my platform grew, the realization did too. "Oh gosh, what have I gotten into? People are actually caring about what I have to say."

Then the devil would jump in and say, "Well, wait. What if they find out? What if they find out you are divorced? What if they find out you made mistakes in your past? What if they find out you are not perfect? They're not going to care what you have to say. They're going to laugh at you. They're going to hate you."

It was terrifying. Past rejection rose up from the ashes and reared its ugly head. But I couldn't let it stop me. Just like you can't let your past stop you from doing what is right.

I had to train myself to have my antenna up for those moments when combative thoughts rise to the surface. I had to learn to actively pause, close my eyes, and think, *That's not who I am anymore. Any mistakes that were made in the past don't define who I am now. None of us are perfect. And if this is my story to tell, I can't let the fear of judgment stop me from spreading this light.*

We've all faced rejection. We have all faced situations that seem nearly impossible to overcome. Big rejections or small, they still carry incredible weight. If we let them, they still halt us in our tracks. Knock the air out of us. Make us feel like we can't take another step in joy.

When I started this social media journey, I became connected virtually with a small group of women. They were also involved in one way or another with home and lifestyle branding on Instagram.

So, when one of them reached out to me, wanting me to link up with them as we braved the Instagram world, I was thrilled. Friendship. Comradery. Helping each other up the ladder. Growing together arm in arm. Perfect. Right?

At the time I had quite a small following, maybe just a few thousand. And this one chick was the leader of the pack, the one we naturally looked up to considering her status. She had around sixteen thousand followers at that time, which—given where I was at that moment—seemed colossal.

We started doing giveaways together. Commenting on each other's posts to help the algorithm. Sharing and tagging each other's stuff. Your regular boost-one-another-up stuff. Everything was going perfectly. And more than the business side, I had found a group of friends. I don't have a lot of girlfriends. The combination of having grown up with a lot of brothers in a fairly secluded childhood and the general busyness of motherhood doesn't allow one to easily or naturally make friendships.

So, when the leader of our little tribe started talking with me about matters unrelated to posts and giveaways, I was happy. When she talked with me on the phone over things she was going through or what life was like in her world, I was glad to be someone in her inner circle of friends she could trust. I enjoyed having someone who called and messaged and supported me, just as I could call and message and support her.

And then suddenly, one day it stopped.

Out of nowhere, it all stopped.

I remember clearly how quickly the transition came. How one day I was texting her after buying an item from her Etsy shop for my husband's birthday, and the next there was radio silence. At first I thought, *Well, of course there's nothing to worry about. She's just busy. She'll get back with me later.*

So I sent another text. And another. And before I knew it, I was not only exiled from this inner circle of gals supporting gals; I was the target of their jests.

Suddenly these women took to social media to write posts aimed at me, jabbing at me and what I was doing. Calling me a fake. Writing thinly veiled comments about how my account was pathetic in one way or another. Even holding up the Bible in one paragraph with verses about the need for kindness and grace, while using the second paragraph to sting me and bring me down.

This occurred not only in their own posts but directly at me. Every time I would post, they'd bully me with an onslaught of negative comments. *Wow, this house is beautiful . . . but not quite as beautiful as the original house I saw for this floor plan, is it?*

Oh, definitely not. The original teal one was much prettier.

They'd use passive-aggressive insults to belittle me in comment after comment, jumping on one another's comments to create a thread of negativity. Eventually even strangers started to screenshot hateful comments they'd see on posts to let me know the women were talking about me.

The cyberbullying was real. By grown women. And it was brutal.

Looking back now, I realize there were red flags. How the first time we ever talked, the leader said, "Honestly, I expected you to be so snobby because you're rich and stuff. But you're not." I heard the chip on her shoulder from the first conversation. While, in reality, we were far from wealthy, given her own financial situation, she saw us as stable.

Her house was smaller than the one we were building. At times she couldn't cover the costs of her portion in a group giveaway, so I stepped in and paid her part. It didn't matter that my family of five was living in a small rental for half of the build and a camper without electricity the other half. To her, all she saw was this big house. And financial security. And probably most of all, the fact that my account was growing and surpassing hers. And she hated me for it.

At least, that's all I can assume, because she refused to ever talk to me despite my messages. Despite how I reached out, asking if there was some way I had offended her and if I could make it right. Despite me trying to get answers and to understand how the tables had so suddenly turned.

For a while I questioned myself and everything I did. It affected the way I posted. Questions flooded my mind constantly. *Does everyone see me as inauthentic? Does everyone think I'm a poser? Is this what everyone is saying about me behind my back?* I second-guessed my motives and my heart. *Why am I here? Why am I showing up? Am I masquerading as a kind person wanting to share tips and tricks and our story when in reality I have only selfish motivations?*

For several weeks I really stumbled. My posts reflected it.

If you look back at my post statistics during that time, you can see that my engagement plummeted. I became afraid to post the way I had been previously, the way that had not only been authentic to who I was but was giving me success. I tried to change everything about the platform that was rapidly growing, the hobby that was on the brink of turning into a major success, to defend myself, to react to the comments that hurt me.

And if I had kept on posting that way, I can guarantee you I wouldn't have made it to where I am today. If I had let my fears run my life, I'd still be struggling to get to fifty thousand followers.

More importantly, though, after some deep thoughts and intro-spection, I reaffirmed that I was on Instagram and was growing a platform for my family. I wasn't doing it to make people think I was somebody special. I wasn't doing it to grow fame for the sake of fame. I was able to reassure myself of those things, feel confident that what the other women were saying about me was inaccurate, and move forward.

But even so, the lack of closure was hard. I was still hurt. I wanted to know what had happened and if I had done anything wrong. I wanted answers. So I messaged the one who always was leading the way for the group, but she still wouldn't respond. And at last I had to decide to let it go. I was going to come back to the platform. I was going to grow. I wasn't going to let their words or actions hold me back. I was going to forgive them. Why? Because the forgiveness wasn't for them. Not really. They weren't responding to me; they clearly weren't even in the know of how I felt.

The forgiveness was for me. The forgiveness wouldn't help them. It would help me.

Facing the Truth About Bullying

When you're holding on to a grudge, when you resist letting go of that anger toward someone, you're just weighing yourself down. As my husband reminded me over and over, I couldn't let them get to me and stop me from doing something I was enjoying, something that was working, something that was my passion. And having Daniel as a source of strength throughout that whole episode meant the world.

Eventually the cyberbullying was so much that I was forced to block them, despite the lack of closure that gnawed at me. But overall I learned a few things through that experience, things that have helped in moments of facing rejection.

I realized that no matter how crazy it seems, it's true that hurt people hurt people. Anyone who reaches out with negativity is more than likely facing something in their own life, past or present, that is shadowing the way they talk to you. Successful people—and not just monetarily successful, but truly successful, those with happy spirits—aren't negative. They're just not.

They want other people to succeed. They want to bring others up.

If you recognize that hate from someone is often a reaction to their own imperfections and insecurities and hurts, then you will be much happier for it. Maybe knowing that will even give you a heart for them. I'm not saying this just as someone on the receiving end of hate either. I have given hate too. I have done and said things I'm not proud of.

I remember a time when I was so insecure. Nobody really knew about the depth of my insecurity, and yet there I was, struggling with my own body image. And I would talk bad about others. I would make fun of people. I would say offhanded comments in hopes of lifting my own spirits about the painful way I perceived myself.

One specific moment was when a girl at work got married. She was a rail-thin, gorgeous redhead, and I remember after she started this specific birth control shot, she started eating unhealthily and gained a ton of weight. And out of my own insecurities, out of my own unhappiness, I thought, *Look at her. How can she be happy?*

I said things I shouldn't have said. I made comments that were rude and, frankly, wrong. Thankfully, I apologized and was able to make amends, but the point is that everything I said behind her back or to her face wasn't really about her. It was just me struggling in my dissatisfaction and tainted view of myself, trying to cover that pain by any means necessary—including hurting others.

But having the support of Daniel and some dear friends has kept me focused—both in big moments and in small. They have been there as a voice of truth when I've gone through something as cosmic as my divorce or as seemingly insignificant (but surprisingly harsh) as a bit of internet drama.

Successful people—
and not just monetarily
successful, but truly
successful, those with
happy spirits—aren't
negative. They're just not.

There's just something wonderful about explaining the situation to an outsider and getting their fresh perspective. It helps you step back from the situation and see things from a new angle. Regarding the social media group, Daniel was quick to say, "Who are these girls, and why do you care? Look at what you are doing. It works. You be the boss you are."

And let me tell you, that meant the world. Little words of encouragement can wake you up.

Good Vibes Only

After that situation with the other lifestyle bloggers, I decided I wanted to be intentional about creating a "good vibes only" space on my corner of the internet. I decided that I was only going to accept those types of comments on my platform and that I would be intentional about only creating positive posts. I created a Good Vibe Tribe and a *Good Vibe Tribe* newsletter where ten different women each month spoke on topics with support and encouragement. I made it a life goal to be cautious with my reactions to my children and husband.

Sometimes hurt people hurt you. Sometimes you are the hurt one hurting people. And if the latter is you, and you don't like the person you see in the mirror, give yourself a pat on the back for recognizing that and making the brave trek toward becoming the person you want to be.

Chapter 8

FINDING HAPPINESS IN THE MIDST OF UNCERTAINTY

After living in a camper for two years in the beginning of our marriage, we made some great strides financially but still were not in a place where we could finance a build of our own. So, having told Daniel's parents we would only live on their property for two years, we struck out on our own and found the perfect rental: an adorable *Southern Living*–style home on an acre and a half at an unbeatable price.

Still, by March 2019 we were coming up on the seventh year we had been living in the rental, and we were feeling it. Paying somebody else's mortgage for seven years. Taking care of somebody else's property like it was our own. Doing the exact thing we had tried so hard to avoid when we were engaged and talking about our dreams for the future. And while we had been successful in using our time in the camper in our early years to meet our goal of saving up funds for Daniel's business and getting ourselves on our feet, we still were more than ready to finally have a place of our own.

The agreement with the landlords the whole time we were building was that once we were getting close to finishing, we would give them a sixty-day notice.

Everything was going along swimmingly until, at the end of March, right in the thick of building, they told us they'd decided to sell the house and we needed to be out in sixty days so they could get it on the market in time for spring. Suddenly we lost our home while building a home. And with month-to-month housing options being both slim and expensive on our shoestring budget, we faced an uncertainty we hadn't expected. What were we going to do? We couldn't get a long-term rental because we would be moving in a few months. On the other hand, we didn't know exactly how many months it would be before the house was ready.

So on top of working our butts off every day on the farmhouse, we had to pack up seven years' worth of living in our house and do it quickly. Selling items. Working through all the stuff in our house for our family of six. All in addition to homeschooling and running two businesses and trying to find a cheap rental.

In the midst of this, new friends of ours again mentioned a camper they had left at a campground in Wisconsin. The campground was closing, and they had to go out and get it. While we had been aware of this camper for a few months, particularly as they had talked with us months earlier about potentially parking it on our land, it wasn't until we were looking around at our meager options that we thought, *Hey . . . we've lived in a camper before. Maybe we could do this again.*

So, sight unseen, we decided to move into the camper. But the plan wasn't airtight. We had to find a place for our family to be in that month between living in the rental and securing the camper. Which is why, for that month, we ended up living with another couple and using their guest suite. A family of six living in a one-bedroom guest suite—a three-year-old, a five-year-old, a ten-year-old, a thirteen-year-old, Daniel, and me. And we made do.

And eventually Daniel drove with his friend seventeen-plus hours to Wisconsin to bring the camper back to our land. Our newest home. There was a queen bed on one side where my husband, our three-year-old, and I slept, a small dining table and kitchen, and two sets of twin bunk beds on the other side, where our daughters slept. We were able to hook it up to electric power, but there was no water. If you wanted to go to the bathroom, you had to go outside to the well, get the gallon jug, fill it with water, pour water into the toilet, do your thing, and flush. We didn't have gas—or the extra energy, effort, or resources to get it working. So cooking was out of the question.

Our days looked like this: We'd wake up, drive to the little gas station up the road to get coffee and breakfast, eat, and get to work. We'd work until lunchtime, and then I'd typically order pizza or get barbecue from a joint around the corner. We had a little fridge in the camper, so on occasion we'd make sandwiches, but for the most part subs or barbecue or pizza was our lunch of choice. Then we'd get back to work until it was dark; look around at our four filthy kids, who'd been hanging out at the property all day; load our crew into the car; take them to Daniel's mom's house to bathe and get them into pajamas; and come back to the camper to figure out what to do for dinner—which, again, was typically barbecue or gas station food or something similar.

But there was one thing that really challenged me during that time.

I hated not being in control.

I had no control over when exactly the farmhouse would be finished. I had no control over the lack of running water for baths for my children in the camper. And I had no choice but to force myself *not* to fixate on the negatives. I had no choice but to force myself to be grateful *every step of our journey* and no choice but to adjust and adapt to every trial thrown at me.

Expect the Unexpected

Nothing can force happiness upon me, just as nothing can force grief. True happiness can't be found in an external situation. We see that with every healthy, wealthy, and beautiful person splashed across the front page who chooses to end their own life, when—to those of us on the outside—there doesn't seem to be a possible reason why. The same is true with the poorest, hardest-working man scrubbing floors while belting a song. It's not external situations that brings joy in the deepest sense.

This outlook helped when, right in the middle of the framing process, I got a call that my younger brother was in the hospital with a startlingly high fever of 108 degrees, his life hanging by a thread. I packed up my kids and drove through a snowstorm to Missouri to be by his side. And I ended up being there two full weeks while Daniel kept working until he could fly out a week later. It was a very emotional time. Stress upon stress upon heartbreak threw me into overdrive.

And yet, that's the way things go, isn't it?

You can't plan for accidents or tragedies or even little inconveniences that end up costing you hours. You can try your hardest and have things run perfectly according to plan for a full week, and then on the eighth day run into something unexpected. Maybe an unanticipated traffic jam makes you miss your flight. Maybe the flu catches you off guard. Maybe a kiddo pops in during that oh-so-important Zoom meeting just to inform you that he threw up on your new white sofa.

We can only plan for so much.

And when it came to building our house in addition to the busyness of our already-packed lives, these types of hurdles hit often.

You know the saying "You don't know what you don't know," right? Well, one of those things for us was our financing. There were parts of the financing of the build that we didn't understand completely. We'd never financed a construction project before. Despite what research we did, we still didn't know all the inner workings, and we came to find out that there was a real wrench

True happiness
can't be found in an
external situation.

thrown into our project: for a significant portion of time we were going to have to find a way to scrape together thousands of dollars *without* the bank's support.

When we closed on the loan, they gave us 15 percent of the money to get us to 15 percent of the build. We had assumed they would provide us with another 15 percent once we were at the 15 percent mark, but instead, according to their policy, you didn't get another draw until you were at 25 percent of the build. So, without warning, we were responsible for coming up with 10 percent of the money between the 15 and 25 percent marks of the build—and faced the reality that this was going to happen several more times throughout the build.

We hadn't known about these gaps. We hadn't known to plan ahead for that.

We had put a big portion down when getting the loan and basically used up all our cash with no money to float us over.

So, suddenly incredibly strapped for cash, we were forced to find alternative means to keep the build going. We had to adapt and get creative.

Learn to Adapt

One thing we tried was finding the biggest-ticket items that counted toward the finishing of the build and doing the cheapest ones first. The bank allotted different percentages. So when your plumbing was done, it counted as a certain amount toward the progress of the build. Drywall was worth another percentage. Electric was another.

We went around the house, trying to do the bigger-ticket items so we could get paid and keep going. And in this moment, we felt panicked. Even Daniel, the dreamer in the relationship, couldn't help feeling overwhelmed when the money situation came to light.

But we didn't have a choice, did we? We could do nothing but put our heads down, step one foot in front of the other, and push on. Every. Single. Day. We had to keep fighting.

Soon enough it became clear that finding and finishing the bigger-ticket items wouldn't be enough. We had to find a way to get more money—and get it fast.

So we stretched even further. Got even more creative. Kept our eyes open for opportunities.

And then Hurricane Michael hit the Florida panhandle, several hours away, and an idea came.

We loaded up the dump trailer and a tractor and drove to Panama City. And for a week Daniel and his crew worked for Florida State University, helping to clear their property. They helped in other ways, too, clearing trees off houses in residential areas. Helping people out. But Daniel also made use of the equipment we had and gained a contract to clean up the university. Meanwhile, my girls and I made meals in our little condo to bring to people I'd connected with through Instagram who were in need.

It was somewhat of a charity event, trying to help people in need after the crisis of the hurricane, but with the contract Daniel was given, it also became a unique way to work hard and work fast using our assets to bring in additional income. And amazingly, it ended up being more than we needed to get us to that next percentage point at the bank.

Meanwhile, we knew we had to keep finding ways to get money, because we were only a few months away from the next financial hurdle we had to jump over.

Enter the door company.

In exchange for a few pictures on social media, they gave us every high-quality door for our house. This was not only the greatest blessing but a mindset changer. Not only would we save thousands of dollars; we realized this was something we could potentially do again. And again. *And again.*

I reached out to *any company* I could think of in hopes of collaboration. Related to *everything.* Tile. Paint. Lighting. Wood. Trim. Water heater. Toilets. Sinks. Faucets. On every aspect of the house, I fought for a connection and collaboration. I researched which companies were in the game of partnering and how to get in contact with them. I made our platform presentable enough that it would win them over. It became my life.

And sometimes they even reached out to me.

For example, one day I got a direct message from a guy saying that another guy he had grown up with had become a furniture designer, and for some reason he thought we would really hit it off. Basically, he felt he should make the connection.

He introduced us, and the friend turned out to be a fantastic high-end designer. We got to talking, chitchatting about life, and eventually he said he was working with an Amish company to design a line of furniture. He wanted to know if Daniel and I would be interested in coming out there to see the whole process, get to know them and their company, and ultimately help design a dining room table that would become part of the product line. And sure enough, they flew us up to Ohio, the CEO picked us up from the airport, and for several days we worked together to design a dining room table—the very one that is now, in fact, in our dining area.

So that's what I did for eighteen months: messaged people all day long. Waited with crossed fingers for responses. Jumped for joy when the occasional brand reached out to me. Worked hard after coordinating with each company to install, capture, and share each product received before the next item arrived. We got tile; we installed it. Took pictures. Posted. We got paint; we painted the walls. Took pictures and videos. Posted. Shared the word on social media. We got a chandelier; we put it up. Took videos. Shared the news. Posted.

I can't even tell you how many times some enormous eighteen-wheeler pulled into our driveway to unload a product. Or how many semitruck drivers we ticked off when they saw our little winding road and had to finagle getting in and out of our driveway. Or how many times we had to drive our tractor out and offload the delivery item ourselves.

But being flexible when the unexpected happens—instead of throwing up your hands or burying your head in the sand—is the key to success.

For example, we did 75 percent of the build with extension cords running to our neighbor's house. To get our power turned on, we had to pay a county fee of $15,000, so when we realized we'd have to tighten our spending, we looked into several options, and turning to generous neighbors to ask if we could use their barn's power was one of them. Waiting until the very, *very* end of the project to get power was yet another way we saved money (though we were careful to pay our neighbors a bit monthly to fund our way).

We had to have an attitude of adaptability. We had to think outside the box.

And that saved us financially for the rest of the build. Looking at what we could do next that counted the most toward building completion, getting the bank out there as quickly as possible to inspect it and get more funds. Laboring hard and long on the house even while Daniel managed a full-time job in his own business and I raised kids. Making final decisions based on products we weren't sure we were even getting in collaboration. Worrying about getting the build done according to the time restrictions the bank gave us, but at the same time relying on collaborations and partnerships to make it happen. Never just saying, "Well, I give up. I see no way out of this" but instead always having the willingness to get creative.

It was time-consuming, exhausting, and overwhelming, but excluding the rare situation, with an attitude of being willing to pivot and adapt, you can do it just like we did.

Chapter 9

ACCEPT HELP

While we did most of the build with our own hands, we still got help for key aspects that made all the difference. We hired help for the Sheetrock and plumbing, asked for help with housing both with the guest suite and the camper, received help with accessing electricity. Neighbors let us do laundry at their house because we didn't have a washer or dryer. Friends would pop in to help here or there, digging footers or putting up framing or installing our air-conditioning unit.

We had incredible help in regard to the kids—the times our parents dropped everything to come babysit for the day or get them out of the work site for a little break and a movie were innumerable. Not to mention the times we dirtied up Daniel's mother's bathroom to get showers at the end of the day while we were living in the camper. There was nothing quite like being exhausted and seeing my mother-in-law's SUV pull in, bringing a hot meal and a helping hand. We are very grateful; we could not have finished the build if not for so many people helping. And there were so many bright stars.

All my kids play soccer. One of my daughters is on a team that has been together over six years. We have that comfortable, casual relationship with one another. We moms get together at the end of the season and treat ourselves to a group dinner. That kind of thing.

So obviously they knew about our build and the moments when we were truly in the trenches. We'd be late for practices or one of the other parents would give our kids a lift to or from a game. And there was one dad who helped us quite a bit. One Saturday after a game, he and a couple other parents volunteered to come over after the soccer game and to just jump in. It was blazing hot, yet one soccer mom was crouched beside me, helping lay the metal sheathing over blocks to keep the termites from coming in. There were hours given with no thought of personal gain or ulterior motive.

Other times my extended family would come over for what we all call Family Holiday—where we gather at one house to do work together. My brother, his wife, their kids, and my mom and dad (who both eventually moved to be closer to us) would come over to jump in and help on the house. My brother built all the hurricane straps. We were all just busy bees.

The point is, we got *help*.

And at first this was a real struggle for me. I am a bootstrapping woman. I want to do it all on my own, whatever it takes. Honestly, most of the work around the house I'm quick to just do myself because I prefer to get things done that way. But while my life typically runs just fine by the motto of, "If you want something done right, you have to do it yourself," there are times I run myself into the ground.

Accepting help? Well, to me it feels downright shameful.

For example, I temporarily hired a tutor to help with home-schooling my kids during an extra-busy season of managing work and home, but I never had the bravado to make it public on social media. Which for me, given I share most of my life on social media, was a big deal.

Why didn't I share? Because I was afraid of the judgment. I feared what others might say. "Oh sure, she homeschools and tries to play this all-in-for-my-kids act, but in reality she has someone else doing all the work."

We play this game all the time as adults, volleying back and forth in conversations with *just how much* we try to pack into a day, until someone has to raise the white flag and say, "Whoa. That is amazing. You are mom of the year."

But then, if your life really is *that* jam-packed, what's more than likely the reality? Either you are doing *all* those *x*, *y*, and *z* things and are miserable, or you have found help and are just not highlighting it.

My friend homeschools her eight kids, runs several companies, has a magazine, and travels to speaking events all the time. I used to hear about her life and couldn't help but think, *How does she do it?* How? And, as our society tends to value accomplishments over calm, I admit I had awe to the point of a bit of jealousy and thought, *What am I doing wrong? Why can't I do that too?*

Then I discovered she has a full-time housekeeper, a full-time nanny, and a chef, and suddenly my perception shifted.

But isn't that just what we're afraid of? Isn't my reaction of "Oh, so that's why. That's no big deal," exactly why I tend to be afraid to seek help? We're afraid that people will discredit the work we do if we get help. We're afraid they will no longer keep us up on that pedestal if we get others to help us manage.

That's the problem in the first place: we put workaholics on pedestals.

When I was a single mom, I worked myself to the bone without any help. And yes, it was a lot, but does that mean I am any less or more valuable now because I have a husband or cleaner or part-time tutor easing the load? Does that mean I should cut the help off and go back to trying to juggle a career and children and home all on my own? No. I have to constantly remind myself that I'm not any less of a person for getting help. It doesn't diminish my strength or work ethic. It doesn't make me a worse mother.

If you can afford a nanny or babysitter or tutor or cleaners or home-delivery meals or whatever, don't feel ashamed about it. Whatever tools and opportunities you can find to make your life

That's the problem in the first place: we put workaholics on pedestals.

easier and lift some of the load off your shoulders, appreciate them for what they are and use them. There's no shame in that. No embarrassment at all.

Yet we all know *those* people. Those friends, like me, who so clearly have their struggles and won't accept help. The sweet friend who ends up with a surprise surgery and won't for the life of her accept your offers to clean her house, cook, or take care of her kids so she can rest. The woman who refuses her parents' continuous offers of babysitting support so she can get a night out with the girls. People who always undervalue their own needs with the thoughts, *I don't really deserve this help. I can do a little bit more. I'm lazy and selfish if I don't.*

If you are one of those women, hear me, because I am you.

One of my biggest strengths is that I'm a hard worker. If I'm at a party, I'd much rather be the girl tucked away in the kitchen, doing the dishes and serving food, than the one socializing. I'm not comfortable unless I'm doing something. So to me, having even the possibility of someone thinking I'm not a workhorse or I'm lazy because I have a housekeeper or tutor or whatever is one of my biggest fears.

I have to work daily to accept that my value doesn't come from how hard I work. That I am more than my accomplishments. That what I need to be doing is loving God, my family, and others well, and whatever it looks like to accomplish that—whether giving it all in some ways or pausing to calm down and take a break during others—is the right thing to do.

I hope you can get to the place that you, too, can accept help.

Chapter 10

OH, MARRIAGE

We had two fights during the build. Which, quite frankly, is crazy because Daniel and I have our fights all the time. But during the build we had just two.

The first was about where the septic system should be built.

And the second one was about the culverts. (If you don't know what a culvert is, it's a structure that allows water to go beneath some obstruction, like a road, railroad track, etc.)

Daniel had a friend who built on a property and had to get a separate permit to put in his culverts. And Daniel was adamant that we had to get this culvert permit, whereas I was googling things and talking to the permit office and saying, "No, it's part of our building permit. It's not going to be a separate thing."

But Daniel was adamant, adamant, adamant. And I was stubborn, stubborn, stubborn. We butted heads because he was certain he was right, and I was certain I was right, and there was going to be no give. (And sure enough, I was right. Hoorah.)

As for the septic system issue, he wanted to put it in one spot, I wanted to put it in another, and I don't recall who was right on that one. (Which means it was probably him because I conveniently can't remember.)

At any rate, the point is, there were times we argued during the build. It was frustrating, it was inconvenient, and at times it slowed down our work, but at the end of the day, we know that a little arguing comes with the marriage package.

After all, why did I get married? So I could have butterfly feelings for the rest of my life? So I could live eternally in this fairy-tale romance? Have financial stability? Companionship? Convenience? Simply to have a dual-parent family with two committed parents ready to start the car for every soccer game and Girl Scout meeting?

Really, at the end of the day, I married Daniel to have someone I could grow with. Susan Sarandon said it so perfectly in *Shall We Dance?* "In a marriage, you're promising to care about everything. The good things, the bad things, the terrible things, the mundane things . . . all of it, all the time, every day. You're saying, 'Your life will not go unnoticed because I will notice it. Your life will not go unwitnessed because I will be your witness.'"[1]

I married him so I could have a person be witness to our lives. Someone with whom to raise my family. Someone to hold my hand across the dinner table in those high moments, and while we sit in silence at the funerals in those low ones. To build a life together.

Before I married Daniel, I watched my great-grandparents. Their marriage wasn't any grand romance novel where Grandma and Grandpa were always caught making out in the corner (thank goodness), but the selfless love they demonstrated toward each other lasted all the way to their graves. They never traveled or had dramatic adventures together. They never dwelled in the lifestyles of the rich and famous. No, their marriage was quieter, one of puttering around a small kitchen together in the mornings, one of listening to the other tell the same story for the five thousandth time and smiling, because that story still brought their spouse joy. Just a sweet little old couple living out their days together in companionship and happiness. Their marriage was the one I looked to as precedent for my own. Their marriage was my goal.

And when I miraculously met Daniel after the hardships of my first marriage, and Daniel knelt on one knee, I knew I had finally found it: my own perfect marriage.

Until our first fight.

Until standing toe-to-toe in the kitchen, arguing till our faces were blue over yet another insignificant thing, and I felt something was terribly wrong.

Where was my sweet, companionable love? Where was the constant companionship and bubbling over of saccharine emotions? *Where was all the puttering?!*

Somehow I had made the mistake of thinking the second I got married the both of us would turn into these mild, sweet folks with nothing but hearts in our eyes, when in reality, we were stubborn. *Terribly* stubborn and willing to go to battle over *every little thing.* We butted heads all the time. We were broke as a joke, with big financial needs. Daniel went from the bachelor life to taking on a wife and two kids overnight. I still had unresolved anger issues from the pain of my previous marriage and childhood, and I also struggled to handle conflict in a healthy way. Every decision was a challenge. Everything we had to spend money on was a stressor. Even our sex life was a disaster and the opposite of what we had both envisioned.

We were stressed to the max and rubbed each other the wrong way at every turn.

By the time our youngest daughter was one year old, I truly wondered if we were going to make it.

I remember packing up my daughters for a road trip with a friend and her kids and picking up a book to read just before we left. We were gone for a full seven days. And when I got back, my mother-in-law informed me of how my husband had come over to their house every day, moping like a little puppy because we were gone.

Call it a stroke of luck or a little miracle, but the timing of that road trip ended up being a reset button for our marriage. That book I had bought was on trying to find a happy marriage. Why had I picked it? Because I was so desperate at that point that I had begun to lose hope. I was miserable. He was miserable. We were both incredibly hardheaded and fought all the time. And the money issues. And the unresolved issues. It was all too much of a mountain to climb. Too hard to get over.

But when I returned, I came back to a man who had gone from experiencing the total chaos of our constantly full house, to the empty home reminiscent of the bachelor life he so willingly left behind not so long before. Daniel didn't want to go back to spending every weekend eating at Outback. He didn't want that life of coming back to an empty house every night. My daughters and I were a handful, yes, but we were good, and we were his. We were worth fighting for.

He wanted his family.

And I wanted him.

Obviously that moment didn't flip a switch so that we never again faced problems or fought, but it was a blessing. A pause to remember that while our financial, emotional, and mental struggles were very real, so were the powerful, sweet, strong moments that made us fall for each other in the first place. And for two people who were far less mature then compared to now (but who still butt heads on occasion), it was exactly what we needed to keep on.

Sometimes taking a step back, taking time to see the forest as a whole instead of standing all day long with our noses up to the bark of one tree, helps us remember the meaning of our marriage and the beauty it has brought to our lives.

No One Can Complete You

Daniel is an amazing husband and father. *Amazing.* He plays with the kids. He works hard. He's loyal. He's faithful. He's a good provider. He's everything I could've ever hoped to find in a husband— practically speaking.

But romantically . . . let's just say we've had to work to understand each other's love language.

He's not naturally a touchy-feely person. He doesn't write handwritten messages on cut-out hearts to leave on mirrors before hopping off to work for the day. In his mind, actions speak louder than words. Providing financial stability, getting up every day to work hard for his family, demonstrating loyalty and faithfulness . . . in his mind all those things are more than enough to let everyone know they are loved.

Every marriage has room for improvement. It took a few years for him to step up to the plate by speaking my emotional love language, and it took a few years for me to lower my expectations and be grateful for all the ways he shows love in his native tongue.

I used to expect Daniel to give me happiness. I thought it was his responsibility to make me feel loved and appreciated at all times, and if he came home and I'd cleaned the house and he didn't say anything, I'd be incredibly annoyed. Why? Because I relied on his compliments and his praise to validate me. I couldn't just be pleased that I'd cleaned the house. I had to be pleased because he was pleased with me.

I had to learn to love myself and do things because I enjoyed doing them, because they were worthwhile to me. I had to do a lot of personal growth to communicate the way we do now and to handle arguments in a mature, healthy manner, including reeling in my sarcasm. I like to make jokes and can definitely get a nasty tone when irked. So if he's lounging on the couch and I'm working hard on dishes, it was easy to throw out a sarcastic, "Thanks for the help" over my shoulder.

And he *hated* that.

He would get so mad at me for talking to him in that voice, and then I'd get defensive and frustrated that he was being so irrational, and then in minutes we'd have gone from a quiet evening to an all-out war.

It wasn't until I realized that he had witnessed people he loved being spoken to in that manner consistently throughout his childhood that I started to piece together why this was a trigger for him. He'd heard others use that tone so often that the effect of me doing the same thing to him was like nails screeching on a chalkboard.

So I made the conscious decision to work hard to delete those sarcastic comments from my language. Really hard. And now, years later, I'm proud to say that old habit died out long ago. Because to Daniel, speaking in love is important. He cannot handle being talked down to or negative jabs, so I had to intentionally uplift him with words of affirmation.

I used to joke and say, "I have to treat you with kid gloves." But actually, it's true. For him words and tone are important, and that's what he needs from me. It took me time to identify his needs and get in the habit of meeting them as best I can. Just as he has worked to identify my needs and meet them.

Old habits die hard, but that's the beauty of marriage: you don't have to get it right in a day. Hopefully, the longer you live together, the more your relationship smooths and sweetens.

Getting Over the Surprise Hurdles

When Daniel and I first met, everyone would tell me how he'd wanted a big family since high school. With a baby brother and sister who were at least fifteen years younger than him, he went through high school with two infants at home. Everyone knew how good he was with babies and how much he loved them, so when Daniel met me and I had two baby girls already, it was perfect. He loved that I

Old habits die hard,
but that's the beauty
of marriage:
you don't have to get
it right in a day.

already had two kids, and he couldn't wait to have even more. And I wanted that for us too. One big, happy family.

So when we were hit with these surprise fertility struggles and miscarriage after miscarriage, frankly, I felt like a failure. I felt like I'd sold him false goods: "Hey, you're going to marry me and obviously I'm able to get pregnant because I already have my two beautiful girls, so we're going to have this huge family together." And then, *bam*. Nothing.

When he got tested and was cleared, we knew this fertility issue was something to do with me. And I felt horrible. I felt insecure. I couldn't help those creeping thoughts of, *He's going to get frustrated that he can't have children. He's going to leave me for someone who can.*

It was crazy, I know, but I truly feared that Daniel would leave. Even though *of course* he had never said *anything* like that, these insecure fears conjured up the idea in my head.

In a marriage we may have invalid fears that crop up simply based on our *own* fears and insecurities. We have to realize what those are and communicate with our spouses early and often so that we don't let an imaginary wedge be driven into our relationship.

There were some years that my grandparents' marriage looked absolutely intolerable. For several years my grandfather was so misogynistic. Barking orders for my grandmother to cook him this meal, iron this, clean that. Complaining that his food was too cold, that she never did anything right, that she had to do it again.

But after several years he changed. I remember seeing the stark difference firsthand. How he came to appreciate her and cherish her, and by the time he died, their marriage was the opposite of what we'd seen years before.

Now pan back to when they were in their fifties, and he was treating her so poorly and so many people could've said, "She should just get a divorce. After all, with the way he's treating her . . ." And while she could've, she chose not to. She made the choice, for whatever reason, to stick it out with him and stay by his side. And in their case, they were able to work through it.

So when the few fights came during our build, when we argued over who was right and pointed fingers at who was wrong, we didn't take ourselves too seriously. Throughout our years of marriage, we've settled into knowing the person who each of us married: a real, flawed, beautiful human being who is more important than any septic system or culvert permit. We are each other's life's witness.

Chapter 11

BUILDING A BRAND
FROM SCRATCH

I first learned about porcelain countertops from a friend who was a kitchen contractor. He said, "They're new. Not a whole lot of people have them in the area. I'm not even skilled in fabricating them yet. They are really expensive to fabricate, so I'd hate to mess them up, but they are a really cool product you should consider."

So I reached out to SapienStone—a high-end porcelain producer—with the hope that they might be interested in providing me the porcelain for our kitchen countertops in exchange for a spotlight on their product. They got my email and put me in touch with their VP. He and I had this long conference call, and it seemed to go splendidly. He said he was going to talk with the team and get back with me. We left the conversation on wonderful terms.

And then I didn't hear from him again.

It was discouraging because we had gotten so far in our conversation and he had sounded so optimistic. But every passing month only made it more clear the answer would be no.

After several months of silence, March hit, and I needed to go ahead and get our countertops. Looking back through emails, I saw that it had been almost a full year with no answer from SapienStone. At this point, I had to admit it. As much as I would've loved to use the porcelain from SapienStone, I was going to have to pay for porcelain. Yes, several quartz companies wanted to partner with me for the kitchen at this point, but I was certain. I wanted porcelain.

So on a Friday I emailed SapienStone and was like, "Hey, I'm just reaching out in one last-ditch effort to see if you might be interested in working with me. At this point I'll even buy the porcelain, worst-case scenario. But I just really would love your product."

The next Monday I got an email from a woman in the company saying, "Hey, I know our VP reached out several months ago, but I wanted to see if it was too late. We really would love to work with you and are hoping there's still a chance."

I'd assumed that the email I sent on Friday went to the right person, but I later found out it went to a person who didn't work at the company anymore. The coincidence was uncanny. As the woman was talking with me, she said, "Our closest showroom is in Naples, which is pretty far for you. We have a private plane, however. We'd love to fly you down so you can look at the options and pick out what you want. When are you available?"

And of course, Daniel and I were *ecstatic*.

We hopped on a plane that very weekend, and in the end, we ended up with porcelain for not just the kitchen but the wet bar, pantry, and master bathroom. Then the fabricator also ended up donating all the other countertops in our house.

It was an incredible weekend and an incredible win.

All because one day a woman sitting on the floor of her rental decided to give that funny little app called Instagram a real try.

How exciting is it that in the day and age we live in, literally anybody, anytime, anywhere can grow a *company* based off their lifestyle? I mean, truly, how crazy is that? Can you imagine our parents getting a chance to do this thirty years ago? I remember my mom at home working so hard, making all these crafts and taking them up to the little gift shop in our tiny town to try to sell them and make a few bucks. Starting your own company was challenging. Even if you did an MLM, you had your little network of friends and that was it. It was so much more difficult to branch out.

But nowadays you can grow anything you want and get it out to the masses, truly millions of people, with just the click of a button. It's incredible that we live in a time where we can achieve all that.

No matter what you're doing, you can benefit from social media if you want to. Even if you have a stable job with a stable income that's as far away from using social media as possible, you can choose to utilize the platform and make money.

Take a nurse, for example. You can hop on TikTok or any of the other platforms and start talking about nursing. You could start a new business discussing nursing tips for getting into the career. It's right there, a free opportunity.

Any stay-at-home mom can use social media for additional income. Whether you want to sell a product, sell information, or even sell yourself because you are a natural storyteller, the beauty of social media is that you can completely do that online. Coming from somebody who went from no knowledge and no degree and no skills on the topic of media marketing, I'm telling you now, you can do it.

Here are some essential tips I've learned along the way.

Jump In

Let's start with the first bright side: it's free! Unlike so many other ventures, it costs you absolutely nothing to give social media a shot. We put a little bit of money into @jettsetfarmhouse in the beginning, around $1,000 spread over a few giveaways, but you don't have to. You can just set up an account, start sharing content on your phone, and go. Simply begin telling your story.

Personally, I recommend you just jump in. Experience is the best teacher, and learning all these things as I went saved me a lot of time and energy. Just do it.

Find Your Focus

I've made it sound so easy, haven't I? While on the one hand it truly is easy, particularly given that it's risk-free to try and that you can jump in tomorrow, on the other hand, some skill is required. We have all seen social media platforms attempt to get big and nose-dive. Nobody likes their content. Nobody is sharing it. Nobody is saving it. Nobody wants to see it. Those accounts are a dime a dozen.

What do they not have that successful accounts do? First off: *a target audience.*

People will say, "You want to find your ideal client, and you want to know exactly who you are talking to." But in the beginning, you don't have to have it pinned down. It may take time to figure out what *you* bring to the social table. What you even *want* to bring to the table. Don't put so much pressure on yourself to get it right immediately.

When I started out, I thought I knew who I was making my Instagram account for: people who enjoyed the farmhouse design style and wanted to follow along on my building journey to learn tips and tricks. So I started sharing pictures about what we were inspired by, where we were getting our ideas from, and broke down every step of the build. I shared our house plans and modifications. I shared about products when they came in. I shared good news and bad news and all the in-between news. And for a while, I thought that was the only thing that set me apart from every other mom on social media. I thought that was all that would help me stand out.

But as I started sharing, people also realized the other dimensions of my life. People realized I had kids. And I liked to cook. And I liked to decorate. And I had overcome a difficult childhood.

And they wanted to know more.

So slowly, over time, I shared more. I expanded.

I am a firm believer that *your brand is you*. Gone are the days when marketing gurus try to tell you that you have to stick to one infinitesimal subgenre within a subgenre for all your posts. That being said, if you *want* to have a specific niche, go for it! If you want to talk *only* about antique rugs and selling the ones you find at estate sales, do your thing. For example, people do this all the time when they showcase their handmade jewelry or pressed flower bookmarks they sell on Etsy.

For those who sit there and say, "But I don't have a niche. I don't have just one thing I want to talk about. I like ten different things," just know that you *can* go outside the box if you want to. You are not forced to talk pressed flowers if you also have an affinity for coffee and French literature. You do you.

This all just depends on your end goal: Why are you on that social media platform and what do you hope to gain from it? If it's to sell books, then you need to target people who want to read books. But if it's more about showcasing your life and earning an income not just from one specific product but from the platform itself and product affiliations, then absolutely feel free to branch out and share more than just one thing.

So, how do you find your audience?

For me, I started from the thing about myself that I believed others would find most interesting. The piece of my knowledge that is most in demand. The modern farmhouse was a big movement, and as we were in the midst of building a house, I jumped on it. I thought that was the one thing about my life that was the most interesting. But as I grew and my brand developed, that niche expanded and I was more and more able to talk about anything because—I'll say it again—I *am* my brand. So long as I kept to the flavor of what was true to me, it worked.

Does this mean I can jump into a totally different aesthetic and start sharing grungy, moody videos of a disco ball in a dimly lit room with no speaking or teaching? Or endless silent videos of a fishing pole in the water, waiting for that catch? Or nonstop videos of me pulling the teen thing and dancing the Renegade in front of the camera? No. Of course not.

Because that's not me. Those are not the things that work for me anyway.

What I do, what is most natural to me, is talk on camera about the things going on in my day and what I have learned. I have expanded from educational building posts to talking about family recipes and how-tos, my childhood trauma and growth, and day-to-day living as the Jett family.

Focus on the thing about you that will be the easiest to talk about and get interested in. And once people get to know you, you become your niche.

Get Seen

I also found other influencers who had a similar message, and I'd go through their comments and engage with those followers. I figured that if those people cared about those influencers and what they had to say, then they might be interested in me and what I had to say.

Of course, you want to already have valuable content when you do this so that when they see your name and come to your page, they find that value. And you have to be doing it all simultaneously to grow. You can't just be making that great content. You also can't just be working to engage with others. It's a perfect blend.

Learn the Rule of Three

There's a well-known rule within social media that your content needs to do at least one of three things: educate, inspire, or entertain. This is your goal, and the more you can accomplish these things in a post or video, the better that content will be.

For example, say you are a mom with three little kids, thinking, *I don't even know where to start.* Start by talking about your kids and the hacks you use in the home. Use affiliate links to share what you are buying, what you are doing.

Give value to those watching or reading your posts.

Could you use that cute picture of your kid eating cereal? Sure. But each time before you post, you have to ask yourself: Why? What would a total stranger get from this photo? What is the point? If you can't answer that question, keep that picture for the baby album and move on.

On the other hand, if the cereal was actually some magical, homemade hack you created from scratch or the bib was some epic life-changer you found on Amazon that every mom dealing with kids taking off bibs and throwing them on the ground would love, then by all means use the photo. That picture, with a caption about what you learned that can help other moms, is educational. Post about it and people will appreciate it.

Be Consistent

You have to be consistent. You *have* to show up if you want to grow.

When I first started, I was posting on Instagram two times a day, seven days a week. Why? Because I knew that the more times I posted and the more I put myself out there, the more likely it was that I was going to be seen.

And it's true.

Even on TikTok it's true.

Like any other business you are trying to grow, it's going to take the most out of you early on. You will likely be able to slow down a bit after you're established, but in the beginning you have to pour yourself into it and consistently show up, providing that value through entertainment, education, or inspiration.

Find a schedule that works for you and your audience and realize that what works for you may be different from what works for somebody else.

You can use tools to help you manage your social media. Apps like Hootsuite, Later, and Loomly allow you to arrange and schedule your posts so you don't have to be on the app all the time. Especially if you have multiple social media platforms. You can schedule content to autopost during a designated time so you don't have to remember.

Consistency is key.

I feel like the algorithms almost come to expect when you are going to post. It may be in my mind, but honestly, when I'm on social media, if I go out of the norm and post in the morning, my posts automatically do more poorly than the times I typically post, between 8:00 and 10:00 p.m. Regardless of whether that's true, I've set up an expectation for my audience, and for better or worse, it's wisest to stick to that and stay consistent. It's like you are training yourself, training the algorithm, and training your audience to know when to expect your content.

Don't let them down.

Don't Give Up

There are probably going to be moments when you feel like giving up.

I experienced success pretty quickly, and maybe because of that you are thinking, *Well, obviously this works for you, Noell, but what about the rest of us who have been pushing and getting nowhere? Clearly I should just quit.* But I'm telling you now, there are loads of people who fight their way into success if they stay in it long enough.

I've been counseling my friend who has been struggling to build her platform for a year. She has been pushing, pushing, pushing every day, and at the end of a year she had only about eleven hundred followers on Instagram to show for it. A few months ago she asked me, "Should I just give up? Is this not for me?"

I asked her, "Are you enjoying this?"

She said, "Well, yeah."

"If you're enjoying it, that's all that matters," I said.

I would say the exact same thing if she had come to me after working in some company for a year and was struggling to feel like she was succeeding. I'd say, "Well, do you enjoy the work? Do you enjoy the field?" And if she said no, then I'd start helping her look for a job elsewhere.

Because at the end of the day, that's what this is all about. Life is short and beautiful, so don't waste it banging your head against the wall of any occupation or side hobby you hate. And the same goes with what you decide to do on social media. Regardless of how poor *or how successful* the content may be, if you don't enjoy it, don't stick with it. The key is to find content that an audience loves *and* that you enjoy. It may take a while, but if you enjoy the platform as a whole, give it time.

The most important thing about all this is to do what you enjoy. If you enjoy decorating, then decorate. If you enjoy baking, then bake. If you enjoy doing calligraphy, then do calligraphy. If you enjoy discussing taxes, then talk taxes. Cleaning hacks. Exercise. Whatever you want to talk about. If you enjoy that and you find joy and happiness doing it, then focus on that.

And that should be your reason for doing it from the beginning. It's not about fame.

If fame is your goal, let me tell you now: you will be unhappy.

Why? Because social media is everchanging. Even if you did reach the top, you could see it all swiped away in a blink if your account gets hacked or the app itself dies out in favor of a new one—which, for the record, happens all the time. Fame is not a reason to do any of this, and if that's your mindset, you need to sit back and reprioritize your life goals. You will be miserable chasing fame if that's all you're after.

Instead, try and think about it as an outlet first. Something you enjoy doing, where you can be happy over the engagement that you get, big or small. Then, as you grow, you won't face such anxiety. Treat it like a job in a field you want to get into, and then if you discover that you don't love the job as it is, don't feel guilty getting out.

Because being an influencer really is a job. Just as there are things about your day job you love, there are also going to be smaller parts of it that are less than desirable. Social media can certainly be monotonous at times, just as doing paperwork can be for someone in another field. I wake up often and think, *Okay . . . what am I going to have to post about today? What's next?* And then, of course,

Life is short and beautiful, so don't waste it banging your head against the wall of any occupation or side hobby you hate.

there are the hours of content I have to make. And then the endless explanations to my children:

"Mommy's gotta go do voice-overs real quick."

"Mommy's gotta post this real quick."

"Mommy's gotta engage real quick."

It's not like there's a point where you flip a switch and everything is easy and fun all the time. In fact, it takes *a lot* of work behind the scenes to make posts look easy and fun.

So in those times of hardship, pause just as you would when you are frustrated at any job. Pull back a little bit to assess the situation. If you get pleasure out of your work, stay strong. It'll just take time.

Think Outside the Box

All of us have days when we struggle to put in fresh content. If you feel stuck, try to think outside the box. Find something totally different and new to try and engage with people.

Here are a few things I tried: I partnered with a store with a much higher following than my own and reached out to them, saying, "Hey, if I buy your product and do a giveaway for my followers, will you share with your followers that I'm doing a giveaway?" So I bought a $200 item from a company with sixty thousand followers to share on my small platform. They, being happy I bought their product and was sharing about it anyway, gave a little shout-out on their own page. You know, just a little "Hey, this girl over here is doing a giveaway of this fantastic product on her page. You should pop over there and join." And to this day, hundreds of thousands of followers later, one of my posts from that experience is *still* the most popular.

I also did things like feature houses with before-and-after shots.

And questionnaires where I'd mix and match kitchens to exteriors and people could chime in with their thoughts.

If you are struggling for content, take a look at what others are doing around you for inspiration. *Not* so you can steal content (never steal someone's content), but in a way where you can see what's working for someone else, something you admire, and twist it to make it your own. More than likely there's something you haven't tried that will be a good idea.

Refuse the Temptation

Growth needs to be organic. Never ever, *ever* be tempted to buy followers instead of gaining them authentically. Yes, technically you can go in and illegally spend a few dollars to purchase bots, but if you do so, you will more than likely be slammed with consequences.

For one thing, the social media platform itself will penalize you. Even those who have done it only one time say that it took *years* to fix the mess they made of their account. One woman I know did this when she first started, tempted by the idea that if you just bought a few thousand bots, then real people would be more likely to follow and engage with your account because you seemed more legitimate. But it jacked up her account so much that the algorithm gave her no credibility whatsoever. When she realized how much of a mess it had made, she tried desperately to fix it and got to the point where she was about to give up. She wondered if it would be better to just delete her account and start all over again because it was such an uphill battle to delete all the fake followers from her account one by one.

The algorithm had essentially pinned her up against the wall. The algorithm knows.

And brands know.

Some companies use software to tell if your followers are fake. They have growth charts and analytical tools to see behind the veil. Also they, like everybody else, have common sense. Seriously, it isn't that hard to see through someone's account.

One company I had built a relationship with reached out to me and said, "Hey, this person is asking for a collaboration and seems to have a decent following, but we're not sure. Something about the account seems shady. Can you take a look?"

What I found was that every single time they posted, they'd gain five thousand likes in ten minutes, then about two hundred more over several hours, and then the post would be done. Every single post. Every single time. If you looked at the person's followers, you'd see several empty accounts or people who followed thousands but didn't have one follower themselves.

It's obvious if you buy followers. Don't do it. Don't take the shortcut for your own integrity, but also don't take the shortcut because it just doesn't work.

As a more legal option, you will also soon discover follow-for-follow giveaways and loops. Someone will privately message you, saying with all the enthusiasm and flattery she can manage, how *happy* she is to have stumbled across your page and how *perfect* it is that *just now* she is running a fabulous engagement loop and she *just so happens* to have a few spots left. And all you have to do is throw forty dollars in the pool for a washing machine giveaway, and together with seventy other accounts, thousands of people will follow you and every girl on there to enter to win. Or instead it may be a follow-for-follow train, and together you girls are going to vow to follow each other and comment to boost each other's posts.

If all of it sounds too easy or too good to be true, it is.

It just is.

What happens when you host that giveaway with seventy other accounts? You may gain a thousand followers with those forty dollars, but all it's going to do is cause you to drastically lower your engagement because when Instagram or Facebook or whatever platform shares your next post with your new followers, they won't give a flying fig about you. They only followed you for the chance to win the washing machine. So either they'll scroll past your post, causing Instagram to think that your posts must not be worth showing your real followers, or they'll unfriend you by the hundreds.

After all, you weren't a person to them. You were just a name on a checklist.

Same goes for follow-for-follow trains. They aren't doing it because they really care about your brand. They are doing it because they want to grow their own. Inorganic, unauthentic growth is never the answer. It's better to have far fewer followers who are actually interested in you and your product than to share your beloved pictures and stories to a blank wall.

The whole point of social media is to find a group of people who believe in you.

Now, if you are trying to collaborate with a smaller group of people within your niche and style, say a group of five, that can be another story. If you can look at those other women's audiences and say, "Yes, if those people were aware of my account, given their interests, they'd be interested in following me too," then yes, link arms with those girls and go for it.

That's a little bit of what I did in the beginning. I worked with a smaller group and we grew. Granted, I spent much more time collaborating directly with retailers and find this to be a better route overall. But powering up with a small group in your field of interest and climbing the ladder together is another great way to do it.

The moral of the story is: don't take the shortcut. Always, always, *always* make it about engaging with your real audience, and not about numbers.

Keep an Open Mind

Half the battle in doing social media to profit in some way is being willing to risk failing over and over again and being okay with it. Keep an open mind and an analytic eye as you go. As you throw out posts and videos, you will eventually start to stumble across content that does better than others. If it works, start doing more of it. If it doesn't, move on.

As you hone in on creating content that you're really enjoying *and* that your audience responds well to, you've discovered a winning combination. If you're that mom of three and you realize that people engage when you talk about packing lunches, start finding cool things on Amazon and linking to those things so people can find them. Then go on Alibaba and find wholesale sources. Then go on Shopify and start your own store.

The point is, you have to keep an open mind when you are creating content so you can constantly analyze what is working and what isn't. Once you determine what works, go with it.

Don't Ignore Analytics

Nearly every platform has an analytics tab where you can see what content is flying and what content is diving. Don't ignore your analytics. You can learn about best times to post, which countries are most represented in your growing following, and—most important—which content gets the most likes, comments, and follows.

There are also apps outside the social media platform that you can use. Personally, I just use the analytics within the social media apps themselves, but there are dozens of good apps out there to help you. Buffer, Hootsuite, Later, Crowdfire, squarelovin, Iconosquare, Keyhole, HypeAuditor . . . the list goes on.

Be Persistent

One of the biggest reasons I see people fail is that they aren't willing to persist. They start out with grand plans to grow, throw up a couple of posts or videos, give it a week or a month or even a few months, and then they give up without seeing any growth. They don't read articles and study analytics. They aren't willing to invest in themselves enough to take a class from an expert or see what works for others and apply it to their own lives. They aren't willing to put in the effort.

Why? Maybe they don't treat it as they would a real job. If you started working as an administrative assistant in a big office, you wouldn't go in assuming you knew exactly how to succeed. You wouldn't be instructed on how to start using a certain Excel sheet format and, after a few tries, say, "Sorry. This is just too hard," and pick up your purse and go. No, you'd expect it to take hours of learning over days and weeks and even months, until the tasks became natural and you were an insider on your trade.

Don't treat social media as just an extension of your family album. If you want to use social media as a business, you need to immediately change your mindset and start thinking about the platform as a tool or a new job.

When I started to use social media, I didn't just stumble into success. I analyzed it to the point of overanalyzing. I researched and read articles. I found people who were marketing gurus on the platforms I used, and I listened to what they said. I read my own analytics. And I didn't expect success to happen overnight.

And you don't need to be active on every form of social media. I don't have Facebook. As I'm writing this book, I primarily use TikTok and Instagram for my business. That's it.

Thankfully we live in an era where there are numerous platforms you can pick from. The important thing is picking one that ideally (1) has opportunity and room for you and (2) is using the methods that'll make you and what you're trying to accomplish shine the most.

For example, some apps are audio only. If you are a salsa dancer trying to inspire people with your salsa-dancing skills and eventually encourage people to purchase your salsa-dancing online class sessions, an audio-only platform won't be the best place for you to put your time. But Instagram, TikTok, and YouTube, where you can showcase your skills through high-quality video? There's the place to invest.

On the other hand, if you love making beautiful, aesthetic pictures and enjoy learning about filtering your pictures using Lightroom, perhaps Instagram is your best bet.

You don't have to be on every single platform. In fact, I encourage you to resist the temptation to spread yourself too thin. Instead, find the platform that will be the most valuable for you, and give it all you've got. It's better to have only two platforms that you're really strong in than to spread yourself so thin that you stress yourself out and barely make a splash.

Adapt to Change

Social media is always changing, and you have to be willing to change with it. You can start your platform thinking your goal is one thing, and that goal can change at any time.

This might be a little different if you have one specific goal in mind, like selling one product or course, but even then the path you take to that goal can change at any time. Being open and willing to research and find new strategies to get out there is truly the key to success. If you're not willing to do that, you're going to be frustrated the second that one app you conquered dies out in favor of another. If you can't adapt, you will fail.

Like with TikTok. Initially I tried to resist experimenting with the new app for a myriad of reasons. It was a kids' app. It wasn't really a credible way to get out there. Wasn't it just silly videos of twelve-year-olds dancing in their bedrooms? But my daughter convinced me to give it a shot, and for her sake—because she was on it too—I tried it out.

And let me tell you, TikTok is *really* different from Instagram. Unlike the posh photos and perfectly manicured pictures of house and lifestyle all over Instagram, on TikTok the ridiculous shine. Often the less perfect the video—the more homemade it looks—the more that video will succeed. TikTok is a land where people can be anything, especially ridiculous.

And if I had just said, "No, no, I think I'll stick with my Instagram-land, where it's safe, thank you very much," I would've missed out on that.

Adapting also involves content. When I first started on Instagram, I shared pictures of farmhouses. I shared beautiful exteriors because someone once told me that exteriors outperformed interiors hands down. I listened to that wisdom and homed in on that, which is what I first became known for: sharing beautiful homes. I ended up in newspaper articles for that. I was talked about because of it. Is that what I do now though? Not at all. Now I share about jelly explosions from my kids and shopping-cart hacks and making biscuits from scratch. I know others, too, who started out doing jokes and skits and fell into being a spokesperson for those with ADD. Others who started out lip-syncing and ended up sharing solely about body positivity as we age.

What is a key difference between being the successful and unsuccessful accounts on social media? The willingness to analyze and adapt.

Don't Be a Copycat

It's a hard call. While it's powerful to look toward other accounts in the same vein as what you're aspiring to for education and inspiration, you want to avoid falling into the trap of either copying them or getting so overwhelmed by how well everyone else does that you get discouraged.

When I first joined social media, I was intentional about this. I was particularly mindful of how it affected my posts when I observed other accounts featuring interior design and home décor and farmhouse style. I didn't want to feel as if I was copying someone. I wanted to let my content grow organically. I wanted to be free from the temptation, consciously or subconsciously, of simply copying someone else and what they did well. And I certainly didn't want to be guilty if someone commented on one of my posts, "Oh, this looks just like what so-and-so would do. You're just copying them."

But at the same time, I knew it was also valuable to be aware of what others were doing in my area.

My childhood wash house in 1989.

Me as a child in church, singing with my family.

The land as we were felling trees.

The land cleared and ready for building.

Our finished home.

Our family making our mark.

Daniel marking out the footers.

The house in the middle of framing.

Planing the pine from our property.

The Jett family in our future kitchen.

Amelia building her own house to match ours. Lots of work, lots of play!

Naptime at the build.

Sanding the walls with Amelia.

Working on social media in my makeshift office.

The porcelain counters from SapienStone in my kitchen.

More counters in my pantry.

The outdoor space before.

The outdoor seating area after.

Maybe it's a matter of intention. If you're looking at other people's accounts because you feel so dry that you have no clue what to do and are going to copy somebody else's great content, then stop. But if you can handle a healthy dose of checking out other accounts to stay on top of what's going on in your little corner of the internet, then good for you. Go learn. Peek around and get a feel for the landscape.

But be careful, especially in the beginning, not to look to other people and copy their voice. It can get overwhelming and confusing when you see all the magnificently creative ways people share about their lives, and if that beats you and gets you down, simply stop. At the very least, wait until you figure out what *your* voice is and what *you* want to bring to the table.

Remember, you are *you* and God has given you your voice and your message for a reason. The world doesn't need another Joanna Gaines. The world doesn't need another Pioneer Woman. The world doesn't need another @jettsetfarmhouse. The world needs you and your memories and stories and life hacks and principles that you can bring to the table. So don't let somebody else distract you or change your tone.

Be authentic to you.

Don't Get Caught Up in the Numbers

Last, remember that you can be successful utilizing social media as a brand without having millions of followers. Though it may feel as if that's the end goal, you would be wise to stop often and remind yourself, "Again, *why* am I doing what I'm doing?"

If you are trying to sell earrings, you don't need three million followers to be successful. In fact, if you are a small business and like it that way, with that many followers at some point you'd get too many purchases in too short of a time and overwhelm yourself.

Whatever your arena, consider setting a reasonable goal for yourself at the outset. Write down a number of followers that would be helpful to you and do your best not to compare yourself with anyone else. It's so easy to compare on these platforms and get down on yourself for not looking as successful as other creators. But remember, comparison truly is the thief of joy, and if you don't have joy, what's the point?

Believe You Can

When I first started social media, I had no idea what I was doing. And I mean *no clue*. I didn't know how to make a post. I didn't have a clue what a media kit was. I had no experience, no technical background. I had barely used social media.

I was not tech savvy at all.

So every single thing I did was daunting. *Every. Single. Thing.*

And the constant temptation was to think I couldn't do this without experience. Who was I? Just a mom without even a college degree and with no special knowledge. I didn't have a degree in marketing. I didn't have fancy camera experience. I didn't have a shop to sell special products. Or some fancy room with a microphone for when I spoke. Who was I? Just a mom.

I didn't think I could be successful.

And I'm here to say, if I can learn how to do it, so can you. You *can* do this. You just have to start.

Chapter 12

TROLLS AND INSECURITIES

If you've seen photos of the inside of our home, you've probably noticed that not a single room has only drywall and paint. Once we started partnering with brands, we got excited and started adding fun features to each room. And for our master suite, I decided to have a pet project all my own.

After I decided to add texture to our main wall, I worked through the negotiations with Cherokee Brick for a selection of thin brick. I had never installed brick before, and as Daniel didn't have the time to help me, I called up my dad.

He helped me lay out my wall and taught me all the basics I needed to know. We installed a guide board where our baseboard would eventually be, then drew vertical lines to ensure my lines stayed straight as I worked my way up the wall. After he helped me get all my groundwork laid out and helped me install the first few rows, he left me to get at it.

I slowly and methodically worked my way up the 160-square-foot wall, using small pieces of HardieBacker as my spacer, measuring cuts and walking outside into the burning July heat to cut the pieces to size using a grinder. Brick dust and sweat coated my skin and hair those days, but when that last piece was finished, I stood back and admired my handiwork with pride.

Another project done.

Another way we were working to make our house into our completed home.

And yet, when I went to share our new project on social media, I can't tell you how many trolls I had to face. How constantly people discredited me when I posted about our wall, just as they discredited me when I posted about anything at all.

You think you actually did any of the work? Please. Nice job trying to take all the credit for your husband.

Okay, sweetie. You can turn the camera off now and let your hubby get back to work.

When it came to social media, I had to learn quick that people were going to hurl insults at me for anything they could think of: being too feminine, too old, too *anything* they could possibly think of to criticize me over. And if social media is something you want to be on—particularly if it's something you gain success in—you're going to have to deal with it too. Trolls and insecurities.

When I first started on TikTok, all I saw when I scrolled were young girls in bikinis showing off.

Thirteen-year-old in pink bathing suit.

Scroll.

Eighteen-year-old dancing in mirror.

Scroll.

Twenty-year-old at beach, flipping hair.

Scroll.

For the first few weeks all I saw were teens dancing in their bikinis, and my immediate reaction was, "What on earth am I doing here? This is not me. I'm too old. I *cannot* dance. I'm not pretty enough. I'm not young enough. I'm not fit enough."

And unfortunately, I realized quickly that this is just going to be the reality: youth and beauty are two of the biggest things people value in our society, and that is most often reflected in social media. Whatever anyone did on there, from singing to dancing to teaching about electronics to sewing recycled plastic purses, they had to show their face and body. And in the society we live in, if you are anything less than the Hollywood picture of model perfection, it's a point against you. To some extent, you will be swimming against the current.

And that was intimidating. But I kept at it, ignored the glaring comments that sometimes hit too close to home, and pressed on. And I'm glad to say it turned out to be worth it, because I grew rapidly on TikTok.

I just had to remind myself of two things. First, the Hollywood definition of beauty is not truth. I am uniquely beautiful as God made me, and while trends and definitions of beauty change over the decades and centuries, God made me as *me*, and I am "fearfully and wonderfully made."[2] Second, just because it will be harder to grow doesn't mean it's impossible. Far from it! With a little searching I found people in my farmhouse-style design niche—twins, in fact, in their sixties—and saw how incredibly successful they were. And as I kept up on social media, I started discovering people who were older, with physical disabilities, mental disabilities, diseases, you name it, and they were all doing something wonderful—reaching the world with their unique stories.

So if you are thinking of joining social media, please know you are not alone in your insecurities and fears. We all face or have faced it. We all have to overcome. You just have to remember that so long as it doesn't start hurting you emotionally and mentally, it's worth it.

We Have Value at All Ages

So you are older? Well, that means you are uniquely bringing more real-life experiences. Remember, you have a story to tell the world. You are given a voice for a reason. You are here with a purpose for this life. And you should not let your age be used as a weapon to hold you back and make you believe you don't have value.

If you have a story and a passion to share with the world, do not let anything hold you back.

You'll Have to Get Thick Skin

If you use social media to build your business, you're going to have to get used to criticism. You have to be intentional not to let negativity affect you.

I see these women respond when someone makes a mean comment on their post. They go out of their way to make a response video of them crying and terribly upset. What do I see from those posts? Only that the negativity got to them. Those types of posts tend to only feed more negativity, showing those trolls that they succeeded, and before long it creates a snowball effect.

On the other hand, if you can ignore the negativity or make light of it, I've noticed that after a while it stops.

Just last week I did a life hack video on cutting pizza with kitchen scissors. And while it was a nice tip for those who actually work with children and weren't aware, people got hold of that video who were not my intended audience.

And they *butchered* me.

Dozens of comments and posts of their own mentioning me. Dozens of duets and stitches where they used my own video for a few seconds on their own posts and then ridiculed me for my idea. Mocking me. Telling me I was a fraud and my tip was such old news it was pathetic. Telling me I didn't belong on the platform. People even telling me I should die.

Horrible, nasty things.

And frankly, for me, I had to laugh.

Because what *can't* I do? I *can't* simply not see it. Yes, I may block

If you have a story and
a passion to share with
the world, do not let
anything hold you back.

people or delete comments at times, but there's always that first time where I see it and it can't be unseen. And unless I want to leave the social media platform altogether and abandon my business, I have to put up with seeing the cyberbullying that happens every single day and be strong enough not to let it break me.

Until the platforms can do something to take a harsher stance on cyberbullying, this treatment on the internet will continue to exist. It's terrible. It's unacceptable. But frankly, it's a reality, and I can't let them win.

The bigger your following gets, the more you will face criticism. Somebody at some time for some reason will be unhappy and judge you for just about anything you do. It truly is impossible to please everyone.

So try your best to ignore the trolls who stumble onto your page. More importantly, recognize what it says about their lives. After all, what do mean, berating comments tell us about the person behind the other screen? Anyone who has that kind of time on their hands to mock me, well, it tells me everything I need to know about their lives.

Even when it's not outright trolls, you will still likely face a more beat-around-the-bush criticism that can hurt just as much. Sometimes more, in fact, because the comments aren't so obviously hateful and outlandish. It may really make you question yourself.

In this case, you also need to understand that not everyone will have gone through the same things that you have gone through; there may be things they just see differently. Just be big enough to understand that they are in a different place and their lack of understanding or empathy or kindness is on them. It's not on you as long as you are well-meaning in your content. Be the bigger person and don't go to their level, tempting as it may be.

Just the other day I posted about a life hack and people were quick to comment, "Oh yeah, I've done that for years." And I just responded with variations of, "Terrific. I'm glad you already know that." But personally, would I ever say something negative and discouraging to somebody else who clearly worked hard to create a video in the hopes of helping others? No. Of course not. That's like walking into someone's bakery and pointing to the blueberry muffins while saying loudly for all to hear, "Wooooow. Those look half as good as mine. I can't believe you try to sell this stuff." It's rude.

But if you can just accept it—and accept that that person apparently is in a place where they need to say those types of things to feel validated in this world—then you will do well. Acknowledge the comments with a simple positive statement, or ignore it and move on.

And remember, you are trying to attract your audience. Anyone who unfollows you is just making room for those who believe in you. I lose hundreds of followers every single day on Instagram (and gain hundreds of new ones), and it doesn't faze me at all. Why? Because your only goal is to reach those people your message is intended for, the ones who appreciate it, and that's all that matters.

Explore Platforms and Methods

Finally, if you just don't want to show your face on social media, you can show content that doesn't focus on your face or body. Various platforms utilize different means. Clubhouse, for example, is audio only. You can always find different mediums to present your content with confidence.

Or you can find creative ways on the typical platforms not to include a visual of yourself, if that's what you want. I rarely include myself on social media, and instead opt for videos and posts focused on the products I'm using or interior design. Others use flat lays—an image shot from directly above—or focus on quality photography of buildings and landscapes and books. You really can be on social media without showing yourself if that's what you choose.

Try your hardest not to let your appearance or your perceived weakness hold you back. Anytime you find yourself feeling threatened or overwhelmed, just knock those words out of your mind. Remind yourself of the unique message you want to bring, and go forth in confidence, proud of wherever you are in life and whoever you have been made to be.

Chapter 13

MONETIZE THROUGH
SOCIAL MEDIA

Before I tell you about making money, let me tell you a story about trees.

After we got the land and cleared the underbrush for our property, we stood there with a bunch of trees smack-dab in the middle of where our house was going to be built. At first we thought we could get a lumber company to come in and pay us for the pine trees, because that's often what they do around here: come in, cut and take the trees, and pay you for the pine. But it turned out we had to have a minimum number of tree inches to justify them coming out, and we just didn't meet the requirement.

So there went that plan.

Then we found out it was going to cost forty grand to have sixty-plus pine trees cut down by a company. Instead of giving in, Daniel just said, "Well, I guess I'm going to learn how to fell trees."

I was nervous at that idea, given my childhood of cutting down cedars on the weekend and one tragic day when my own father got the rope caught in another tree and nearly lost his life when one fell on him. So my reaction to Daniel was more of gritted teeth and saying, "Are you sure about this? My dad had years of experience and still got hurt. Please be careful."

But Daniel was insistent.

And sure enough, he went on YouTube and watched every video he could find. Learned all the terminology. All the cut styles. Everything he needed to know to do it himself. He went back to my dad and got any advice he could. Got the chain saw. The face apparatus and protective gear.

And before we knew it, there we were, out on the four-wheeler, heading onto our property with chain saw in hand. He'd saw to just the right angle, and then we'd hook a rope around the tree, pull the rope back to the four-wheeler and tie it off, and I'd sit on the four-wheeler, giving that extra tension and guidance for the tree to fall the right way.

Once a tree was down, we'd stack it with the others, and once the sixty-plus trees were down, we hired a portable sawmill company to help us turn all those trees into lumber. We eventually used the boards for our front porch, the siding for our watershed, and the mantel on our fireplace, and we still have more left over for future projects.

We did $40,000 of work ourselves armed with nothing more than YouTube videos and reaching out for advice. We made it happen, even though it was scary and intimidating and at one point it seemed it couldn't be done.

Maybe that's how you feel about the idea of monetizing through social media. Maybe it sounds so advanced and complicated in an area you have no experience in, and your temptation is to leave such activities to the business-savvy people.

If you think that, don't. *Anyone* can monetize through social media.

You just need to know which tools to use. And I'm here to show them to you.

Instead of thinking of social media like you would, say, driving down a straight road from point A to point B, think of it as a highway that splits off into a dozen different directions with a dozen different exits. All exits are accessible to you, and you can get back on the highway to take another exit at any time.

That's what makes social media even more powerful than doing something like opening a candy shop downtown. Instead of opening one store in one location and putting all your hours and energies into getting people into that one store to purchase that one set of items, you are using your time to build up a dozen opportunities to profit through a dozen or more avenues.

Let me break it down.

Getting Paid

Once you have a certain number of followers and meet a few minimum standards, you can simply post videos *about anything at all* and get paid based on your video views on TikTok or YouTube. And I'm not talking about this being an opportunity only for those who have millions of followers. I'm saying that at the time of this writing, if you have ten thousand followers and at least ten thousand views in the last thirty days, you can start getting paid. The more engagement and views you have, the more you get paid. In December 2020 I received a bonus from TikTok for doing a certain number of posts for the month. The posts didn't have to be about building houses. They could be on anything at all, and the platform itself paid me.

Affiliations

There are several affiliate programs: CJ Affiliate, ShareASale, RewardStyle, Amazon Associates, Rakuten, ClickBank, and ShopStyle, just to name a few. Find one that works for you, research those with the most competitive commission rates, start sharing about things already in your home, and you are in business.

You can use affiliate links where a company will pay you for directing traffic to them. When you make a post, you can simply write the link to the product you are showcasing in the caption or in your bio or in your paragraph somewhere, and whenever somebody clicks on that link and purchases something, you will get a percentage from the company itself. Sometimes there is even a "cookie life" for that click. Say that person didn't purchase the item at the moment they clicked, but thirty days later you *still* could get paid a commission for that link! And all you did was showcase a helpful item that your audience is interested in anyway and include a link so they could easily find it. A win for your audience wanting to know where you got the item, for the company happy you are guiding followers to them, and for you getting a percentage while keeping your audience engaged.

In-Kind Collaborations

Of course, you can also do what I have loved doing: collaborating with companies that simply sent me product in exchange for me sharing about it. Some creators I know refuse this type of collaboration, but that was how I got over $70,000 worth of doors when I first started. Did I receive their offer of free doors and say, "No way. Only if you also pay me." Absolutely not! I was thrilled for the product itself and more than happy to share.

Product Line

Plenty of people out there go into the business of social media knowing exactly what they want to sell. They have that local candy shop downtown but want to start shipping around the world.

Then there are people who grow such a following that they can sell anything, anything at all, and monetize it. I see lots of young people making T-shirts on TikTok with something as simple as their name in plain font across the front. Really, anything can work. You can use sites like Alibaba or AliExpress to source things from a wholesaler and make your own line.

You can also do a product line with another company. For example, I did a collaboration with a local company in which we designed boxes with candles and coffee and tea towels inside. Even on a small scale, you can work with other established companies to sell online.

Courses

Do you enjoy cooking? Do you want to share your interior design tips? Use your talent and design eye to entertain everyone—and also throw in that you offer private design services. People will pay for coaching for everything you can imagine. Marketing. Singing. Creating excellent résumés. You can be an author coach, helping aspiring authors develop proposals and learn which agents and editors to pitch to. You can be a life coach. You can do virtual chef sessions. Truly, just about any area you can think of, you can teach one-on-one virtually or in groups and get paid a significant amount.

If you don't have time or interest in Zoom sessions and phone calls, you can create online e-courses through short books or handouts or PowerPoints or videos and sell it as a downloadable item.

Surprising and Unusual Ways

The more you delve into the great and wonderful world of social media, the more opportunities will crop up—even really unusual ones. Someone once paid me $500 to stick a link to their website in a blog post. So even if you don't know how you will utilize social media now, know that eventually the more you do it, the more you will find ways to use it.

Paid Collaborations

Another powerful way to get paid through social media is by paid collaborations with companies. They can reach out to you, but you can also reach out to them. There is a bit of an art form to this, so I'm going to walk you through it. Here is an example of what a company might send to someone they want to collaborate with:

Hello there!

We came across your page and love your content!

We are currently looking for like-minded influencers who appreciate quality home products that make living easier. We think you would be a great fit for our product!

Please see the attachment below and check out our page. If interested in sharing about high-quality, soft, hypoallergenic organic sheets that will transform your sleeping lifestyle, we would love to send you a product.

If this sounds good to you, just let me know and we can work out the details.

Sincerely,

Best Rest LLC

If I were coaching her on how to respond, here's what I'd say: First, say something flattering to show you actually read the email. I'd respond with something like: "Thank you so much for reaching out. I appreciate your kind words. I love the idea of partnering with a brand that focuses on being eco-friendly and has such wholesome values."

Then at that point you should mention the media kit that you have attached to your email, which I will discuss below. If you don't have a media kit, you can also say, "My rates start at . . ." and provide whatever number is wise. To know how much to ask for, I suggest referring to Influencer Marketing Hub—it'll tell you the general number influencers at your following level would charge. They cover all the platforms with a standard rate per thousand followers.

You may want to have some qualifiers. For example, you may have to work through who owns rights to the photos or how long the company is free to use them. The brand may also want you to post a certain number of posts or videos that are above and beyond the normal number, and you can comply with a raised rate.

I recently worked with a plant company, and they said they needed a minimum of three hundred thousand views to make it worth what they paid me. So with that qualifier, if I hadn't gotten that many views on the first try, I'd have to make another video until I got there.

After you send that email, it may take some haggling, but eventually you will come out on the other end with or without a deal. Be aware that if you get that deal and they start to tack on multiple expectations you hadn't planned on, you need to go back and discuss your rates for those things as well. You do not owe them excess time, energy, posts, or videos just because they gave you their product. Make sure you represent yourself fairly.

If you don't feel comfortable giving your rates, you are always welcome to ask them, "What's your budget for this?" Whatever they come back with, you will then have to make a choice. *Is it worth the $200 for me to do whatever they are expecting of me?* You decide.

And whatever you do, don't undervalue yourself. *Anything* you do is of value. If they ask you to include a hashtag, it has value. Put content on your story? It has value. Creating a carousel post? It has value. Every step they add to what they are asking has value. So if you find yourself in a position where they originally said they wanted a TikTok video, and then they follow up and want the TikTok to be put over on Instagram, too, don't automatically do it. It has value, just like your TikTok does, and it doesn't even matter if it's the same content. It's a different platform, and it's your time and energy that have been invested into building those platforms, and you deserve compensation for your work. They should pay you for exposure to your audience.

And one thing to consider: Typically anytime you are posting anything in a collaboration, you are decreasing the value of your brand. Just a little bit. So it is important to weigh out every collaboration and ask, Is this worth cheapening my brand just a little bit?

Media Kits

In the beginning I had no idea what I was doing. Remember that. Nobody starts off as an expert, so don't feel like you are instantly behind for not realizing your full potential. I had no idea collaborations were a thing. I had no idea you could get paid *at all*! I started out doing social media as a creative outlet and then learned as I went.

Consequently, I didn't immediately start out with a media kit. It was only after the door company reached out to me asking about a collaboration that I realized I should pull myself together and look professional. At that point I had started listening to podcasts and was doing some reading, so I had gained an awareness of what influencer marketing was and what I could get myself into.

A media kit is basically a snapshot that quickly tells brands who

Whatever you do,
don't undervalue
yourself. Anything
you do is of value.

you are, what you do, your analytics, and what your demographic looks like. You can also include a rate sheet, but technically a rate sheet is separate.

So if I'm taking a trip and talking to a company about receiving free lodging in exchange for exposure on my platform, I may send the company a rate kit so they are aware of my typical rates, but I'm not necessarily expecting payment.

There are plenty of places where you can use a template to create your own media kit. I recommend you head over to Canva to create yours. They make it easy with a media kit template, and you can change the colors, backgrounds, fonts, pictures, and so on, to make it your style. But if that seems too daunting, you can always hire someone (for example, on Fiverr.com) to help you make one. The biggest recommendation I'd give if you go that route, however, is to make sure you order a kit where you can customize the numbers yourself at any time.

I made the mistake of hiring a local brand to make a kit for me, and every time I needed to update my numbers (which in my case has been weekly), I had to email them and wait for them to fulfill my change request. It was so frustrating that eventually I had to give up on that kit and get a new one made. Make sure that whatever you use is easy to update as your numbers grow and change.

A Word to the Wise

As you get started down this winding road of social media, know that it can get tricky. Sometimes shady people and corporations may reach out to you, trying to scam you with high and unreasonable demands—or even worse, simply trick you into buying their products thinking that somehow you'll get paid back in the end.

For starters, don't ever buy the product unless you were planning to in the first place. Hundreds of companies you've never heard of before will prey on social media newbies, reaching out to young accounts, telling them that their content is flawless, and "offering" them the opportunity to buy fifty-dollar yoga pants here or thirty-dollar sunglasses there, stating that they will make all that money back and more when people use their link. The problem is that you, fresh and new to the world of social media, may not be fully aware that having an account with one thousand followers and few engagements isn't going to get you the results you need to get that money back. Not enough people will see your post, and then you will be out the money and feel like a chump.

So rule number one: don't buy something that someone messaged you about just because you "might" make money on it.

But if someone reaches out and they have a product you love and would probably be buying anyway, then sure, go for it! A tile company once reached out to a friend of mine and said they'd give her a 10 percent discount to buy their tile plus an affiliate link, and she was happy to do it. She was going to be buying that tile anyway. It was certainly worth it.

When to Monetize

You need to be cautious about *when* to start trying to monetize.

If I had started trying to sell home goods to people on social media the second I started three years ago, do you think I would've made that much money? Probably not. If I had started trying to sell things to people right out of the gate, it not only wouldn't have done very well but my audience would've been frustrated and felt advertised to.

Instead, I took the approach that my sole goal was to educate, inspire, or make people laugh. By growing my brand based off those principles and not to make a quick buck, I began earning people's trust. My brand became established. After gaining people's trust, I was able to start monetizing through affiliate links and collaborations.

So take your time. Wait until you have established your brand, and then wait for the right collaboration or product that fits you. Be authentic.

Just Start

Even though you may have imposter syndrome or feel overwhelmed in the beginning, know that most of us also felt that way when we started out. Just start. Be adaptive and teachable and realize you don't have to have all the answers in the beginning. It doesn't matter how bad the content is. How bad the editing is. How little you know. How wrong you got that last post.

Just start, because that is the biggest difference between those who are going to be successful and those who won't. People get so overwhelmed thinking they have to get PhDs in something before they can begin. But if you are willing to put yourself out there, willing to fail a few times, you will find yourself so much more ahead of the game.

It's as simple as that: just show up.

Same with consistency. Just show up.

Be present. Be there for your audience. And that's how you will make a great start.

Chapter 14

PATIENCE AND PEACE

The oven was an exceptionally expensive appliance in our build, and the dream one I wanted we simply couldn't afford. Reaching out for a collaboration yielded nothing, so instead I decided we would have to wait to pay for the real thing. In the meantime, Daniel was doing a remodel for a customer's house, and when they wanted the old appliances removed, we were able to pull an old double oven out and stick it into ours. It was too small for the space. It was loud. It was beat-up. But it was free, and it worked.

And for a year living in our house, that was what we used.

Until one day Daniel found the exact one I wanted in a scratch-and-dent shop three hours away and surprised me by driving down there, picking it up, driving the three hours back, and installing it—all without me being aware.

It was the best surprise.

Perfect. Beautiful. Matched my cabinetry wonderfully. And well worth the wait.

And while we did celebrate that sweet moment, I think I should make one key point clear: if none of this had ever happened to our family—not the ovens or the followers or the farmhouse itself—we would still be happy. We would still be the Jett family. We would still be us.

Our farmhouse build and the success of our brand itself through social media have been amazing; it's truly been a dream come true. But the journey to get to where we are today was a decade long, and if we hadn't loved our lives right in the thick of it all—both on four-wheelers yanking on trees in one-hundred-degree heat and in kitchens of porcelain while covered with the makings of blueberry pie—then what a sad waste that would have been.

We as a family have made it a priority to love our life every step of the way. To prioritize taking time away (six weeks each year, in fact) just to focus on spending time together. To work hard and play hard. To know that every good thing can come or go in a blink, so we might as well fully appreciate each moment. And to be content where we are, as we are, while pressing on with patience.

I can see how it could be easy for someone following our story on social media to think that our house was perfectly finished by the time we got that stamp of approval and our certificate of occupancy. But the reality is, I didn't have to point my camera toward what wasn't finished. My videos didn't have to paint the full picture of every angle of every room. Which is why for the first six months I didn't show the living room that was completely void of furniture because we were waiting on a partnership to come through. I didn't show that wall of plywood where we hoped the fireplace would one day go. Heck, it wasn't even until this past weekend—already having lived in our house for a year and a half—that we finally filled all the holes in the ceilings throughout the house with actual speakers.

We still have trim to paint.

Decks to finish.

Crown molding that needs to be put up.

And by the time we get all that done, I'm sure we'll have our share of repairs and new ideas that will keep the to-do list flowing.

I don't know that it's ever really possible for a house to be truly "done"—especially when you are the ones doing most of the work yourselves. In fact, COVID-19 hit right around the time we moved in, and not doing a housewarming party due to the pandemic seemed somewhat fitting.

But if I'm not content with where I am at right this second and with the status of my home as it is, then I'm never going to be. And I had to learn that; it's not something I just knew.

I watched my dad lose his health when I was a child. I knew what it was like not to have the money to just go to the grocery store and get basic needs. I was miserable in my childhood. I was miserable and, for a long time, bitter. And that bled into my adulthood. Always thinking, *Okay, once I'm in this better position, it'll get better. Once I'm here, I'll feel better.* And frankly, it never turned out that way.

There's an old saying that "a change of geography does not create a change in character." And as someone who has moved roughly twenty-five times since I left my parents' house—jumping from dorm room to apartment to apartment to dorm room, heading back to my parents' house and then on to a new apartment—I can verify the truth of that saying. I would constantly exhale in the midst of a move and tell myself, "Okay, now. *Now* it's finally going to be better once I get there. I'm going to do better as a whole. I'll feel better and complete." But then, every single time, I'd get in my new place and look around, asking myself, *Where is your happiness? Why aren't you happy?*

It wasn't until I lived in the camper for the first time that things changed. We were living on Daniel's parents' property, and I began to see how I reacted to things. Noticing how every time I thought something was going to be great and the be-all and end-all and I'd reach that milestone, and yet nothing changed for me emotionally. There was a pattern of discontentment. I always kept rushing toward the next big thing, never pausing to stop and enjoy the moment.

I rushed through life. Rushed through sweet moments because I was so busy thinking about what could happen next. Not paying attention to the little things.

At that point I really started to work on myself. My first step was to slow down, as I saw Daniel's parents do. I started to take my time

If I'm not content with where I'm at right this second and with the status of my home as it is, then I'm never going to be.

on things. Do something correctly with all my attention and enjoy seeing the task completed. Appreciate the moment. By doing that over and over, it became a practice in my life. It was a big first step in helping me live with peace.

I will never forget one day when I was putting away an extension cord in the detached garage at Daniel's parents' house. How I was raised and how my nature preferred to do it was to just throw the cord in the corner and walk away, but I knew his dad would want me to roll it up and put it back properly. I flung it in the corner anyway. But as I started to walk away, I paused. *You know, he would want me to do this the right way. I shouldn't just rush toward the next thing.* And so I did it. I walked back, forced myself to appreciate the simple act of seeing a task completed in an orderly fashion, and started myself on a journey—that very moment—toward slowing down.

At its root, contentment is all about the right mentality. Finding the little things to be grateful for—our health, our family, the freedom we have in this country. These are the things that matter. These are the things that at the end of the day bring us joy.

You can't wait for something to make you happy. Or fall into the trap of believing that once you get that one thing you will finally be content with your life. Grab that joy now in the trials, in the journey, in the mess, and hold on to it through all life's ups and downs.

And if and when your dreams come to fruition, I hope it's icing on an already beautiful cake.

Afterword

CHASE YOUR DREAMS

Just a few days ago I came across this old email from my father, dated from when I was a sophomore in college, living in Oklahoma City.

> I'll say this. The opinion of most people about you is that you are a little wild. Some folks are just waiting for you to mess up so they can say, "I knew she would mess up. She's always a troublemaker."
>
> I'm taking one of the biggest risks of my life in ministry by allowing you to stay. I just want you to keep in mind the high cost of low living. I love you and always have a place in my heart for you—you're my flesh and blood; how could I not forgive you if you mess up? But do right. If you break your mother's heart, I'll wring your neck.
>
> I don't agree with everyone about you . . . but you can make mistakes . . .

Imagine how it felt hearing things like this for your entire childhood. How people were watching you. How they were judging you. Chiming in—sometimes quite loudly—to point out where you had failed. Pinning down expectations on the way you have to act and live. Telling you that you can only go to this line in life and not a step further.

For the record, I did make mistakes shortly after this email was written. I was stubborn and hardheaded, and just like everybody else in the world, it turns out I wasn't perfect. Nor will I ever be on this side of paradise.

What I am challenging is that over and over, whether in my childhood or even as an adult, people have tried to inform me of my boundaries. Telling me that I needed to get a degree to market anything. Telling me that as a woman I wasn't allowed to attempt working outside the home, much less in jeans. Telling me that I wasn't skilled enough, educated enough, wealthy enough, connected enough, young enough, driven enough, smart enough, pretty enough—to be on social media, run a business, and build a home.

But my experiences cry bull.

When we started our house build, we had to get an appraisal from the bank before we could get the loan. The bank did this so they could make sure that at the end of the build the house would appraise for whatever amount of money we were trying to borrow. It was a safety net for them. And when we got our house appraised before we started construction, it appraised for $400,000.

At the time we thought that was a little low, but we didn't fight it because we only needed $325,000 to complete the project. At the end of the build, the bank came out to appraise it again. This was supposed to be standard procedure, something they had to do before they could roll the construction into a traditional loan. It was supposed to be nothing but a bit of paperwork, and everyone could be on their way.

But the house appraised for over a million dollars.

And basically, the bank panicked and started pointing fingers. They accused us of bribing the appraiser, asked us if we had paid him off to give a higher appraisal so we could then turn around and sell the house for more money. They accused us of lying to them about where all the stuff in our build came from. They accused us of having liens on the house and not telling them.

Our loan officer knew what was going on, having watched our process and how we had harnessed the power of social media to get hundreds of thousands of dollars in materials. She tried to explain it to her supervisors but got nowhere.

So I got on a conference call with the president of the lending division, who'd been with the bank for decades. She came on the phone with this attitude like she's about to have to deal with this manipulative, lying person. To her credit, had I not experienced firsthand what had happened in our build, I would've had suspicions myself.

But I said, "Hold on here, ma'am. We aren't trying to pull anything over on you. This has blown us away just like it's blown everybody else away. Obviously if we had known it was going to happen, we would have told you guys in the first place."

I ended up having to educate her on social media and Instagram and marketing and collaborations, and in doing so I had to say, "Look, this is probably not going to be the last time you deal with something like this. This is happening more and more, so you might want to adapt your ways and change your thinking."

In the end, I had to help the president of this division see not only that I could, in fact, break out of the acceptable norms but that she could break out of that old-fashioned mindset as well.

People are always going to try to pin restrictions on you. People are always looking at the way "everybody" does something and assume that just because it has been done one way in the past, there is no alternative. Then they'll encourage you to stay in your lane. To follow the unspoken societal rules that have been handed down for generations.

Well, here's the thing: If you have passion for something, try it. Give it a shot.

Whether it's with how you mother your children, pick your career path, build your home, whatever, you have freedom to think outside that narrow box. No matter what your dream is, large or small, if that is your calling, I'm cheering you on. *Go for it.*

I hope you feel confident to pursue being the person you were meant to be and to fulfill the dreams you were meant to fulfill. I hope you take time to slow down, appreciate each moment you have in this beautiful life, and ask yourself, "Why was *I* placed on this earth? What is something I was meant to achieve?"

And whenever you get those answers, I hope you blaze forth toward it, with much endurance and much flexibility and much patience, and a whole lot of joy along the way.

A Note from the Author

It's sometimes very difficult to find words that accurately explain a situation or relationship. And I can't pretend that my family's relationship is perfect or that we have found total healing, but it is a work in progress.

Have you ever met a perfect human being? Someone who never made a mistake or a decision they regret? I know I have made more than my fair share of mistakes as I have stumbled my way through life. While sometimes boundaries do need to be defined and lines drawn in the sand for the sake of our mental well-being, when possible, choosing to forgive and love each other—even though we may not understand decisions that were made, or actions taken—is a necessary step to allow healing and to help us find peace in our own hearts. I've seen first-hand how much damage can be done to a family if people refuse to forgive and know that, when possible, it's worth choosing love. Above all, I'm eternally grateful for the positive things my parents instilled in me: a hard work ethic, drive, determination, and above all, love.

Mom and Dad—you both inspire me in ways you will probably never truly realize and I'm so grateful you are my parents. I love you very much!

Reader, I hope my story inspires you to realize your dreams, find forgiveness, and always chose love.

Questions to Ask Yourself

Chapter 1: Rich or Poor

1. If you could imagine any life for yourself, what would it be? Write four tangible things you would like to achieve to have a better life.
2. Who is someone you know who is living a life you aspire to? Ask them, "How did you get to the place you are now? What wisdom can you give me?"
3. Think of a time when you failed. What did you learn from that experience? How can you use that lesson to propel you forward instead of letting the failure defeat you?
4. Do you feel you are working hard but getting nowhere? How can you work smarter, not harder?

Chapter 2: When the Going Gets Rough

1. How have unhealthy religious experiences affected your relationship with God? With others? With the way you see yourself?
2. When have you had a low moment and felt like giving up, but didn't? What gave you the strength to press on?
3. Have you ever been told that you were not enough based on your gender alone? That you didn't have the freedom to pursue things because of your race, gender, religion, or something else? How did you handle those situations?

Chapter 3: Finding Relief in the Midst of Discouragement

Check the boxes of any of these you can answer yes to:

☐ Do you live on an emotional roller coaster, where one day you can take on the world and the next you feel like you can't get out of bed?

☐ Have you ever felt so low you've contemplated taking serious action against yourself?

☐ Do you ever struggle with seeing only the negative in life? Wondering why you can't get out of your slump?

☐ Has anyone in your family tree had depression or symptoms of depression?

☐ Do you have everything—the home, the finances, the stability, the goals—and still feel empty? Still wonder, "What's the point of it all? Why am I not happy?"

If you checked any of these boxes, take a few minutes to look up a mental health professional in your area. You don't have to call yet. Just peruse their website. Read reviews. Do your research. And if you are willing, consider taking the next step and making the call. You just might look back on this moment as the one that turned your life around.

Chapter 4: Learn on the Job

1. For Daniel and me, success in our career path means financial stability, doing our passion, and having freedom with our time. List three to five things that characterize a successful career to you. Looking at the list you made, does your current occupation fulfill your goals?

2. Do you ever feel like you are less valuable because you missed out on a college degree or other traditional achievement?

3. If you are hoping for a new career, can you gain this career without schooling? Are there alternative programs you can take advantage of?

4. Is there an expert in that field whom you can shadow?

Chapter 5: Instagram: Where It All Began

1. What three topics could you talk about for hours on end?

2. Which of those topics gives you the most joy?

3. If you were to start using social media as a means of business, what would be your end goal?

4. What are your strengths? Are you funny? Do you teach well? What social media platform best corresponds to those strengths?

5. How well do you handle criticism? How can you guard your heart when people on social media try to hurt you?

Chapter 6: Beauty on the Inside

1. Have you ever experienced someone treating you differently once your looks or things you owned looked more culturally appealing or high-end? Have you experienced the opposite? How did you handle the situation?

2. Has there ever been an instance when you judged someone else, even without meaning to, based on things they owned or the way they looked? If yes, why?

3. How can you guard your children's hearts and minds so they aren't deeply hurt by the judgment of outsiders? How do you teach them to love themselves?

4. Have you ever thought, *If only I had_____, I'd be happy,* and then once you got it, instead of being content you just wanted something else? How do you battle discontentment?

Chapter 7: Dust Yourself Off After Rejection

1. Write down a time when you said (or thought) something negative about somebody else—whether to their face or behind their back. Why did you say it? Were you dealing with something in your own life that could be directly related to the way you thought or responded to the situation?

2. Write down a time you were senselessly hurt by somebody else out of the blue. Why do you think they did it? What indicators in their life could have hinted that something was wrong?

3. After facing the above rejection, did you fear that everyone else thought and felt the same way about you? How did you or can you overcome it?

4. Is it easy for you to let conflict go without closure? What can you do next time you're in a similar situation that will make it easier for you to move forward in peace?

5. Think of the last three conversations you had with someone in your family, someone outside your family, and someone at work. Was each a pleasant conversation? In one word, how would you describe the overall vibe of each conversation? Now put that label on yourself and ask, *Is this who I want to be known as? A _____ person?*

Chapter 8: Finding Happiness in the Midst of Uncertainty

1. How important to you is having a sense of control? Are you the type of person who makes a ten-year plan for your life? If so, how do you react when your plans go off the rails?

2. What can you control in your life? List five things you can control and five things you can't. How do you feel about the things you can't control?

3. List one hundred things you are grateful for, as significant as your eyesight and as small as the coffee mug in your cupboard. Keep that list close for moments when you feel discouraged.

4. Has there been a time when something bad happened and you couldn't understand the reason, only to discover years later that a positive thing came directly from the experience? A key way your character was shaped or perhaps something that led to that dream job?

5. Who is someone you have seen generally contented through both good times and bad? Consider asking them why they have happiness through thick and thin.

Chapter 9: Accept Help

1. Do you ever admire those who have so many activities on their plate that it sounds impossible for them to actually complete them all? Why?

2. Do you have a hard time accepting help? List several possible reasons why it is difficult.

3. What is the first thing you think about when you wake up in the morning? Do you ever wake up with anxiety about all you have to get done?

4. If someone were to offer to bring a meal to your house after, say, an illness or minor injury, what would you say to them?

5. What is one great thing that could ease the load in your household right now? How can you make that happen?

Chapter 10: Oh, Marriage

1. Do you have a particular couple you look up to? What characteristics are in their relationship that you admire?

2. Do you have too high of expectations for your spouse? Do you have extraordinarily high expectations for yourself?

3. List three things your spouse does well. Find ways to specifically voice your appreciation over the next week. Ask your spouse to do the same for you.

4. While hardships in marriage are impossible to avoid, some things in marriage should never be tolerated. Do you ever fear for your life or safety? Is your spouse physically hurting or threatening you? If so, immediately seek alternative shelter and safety and professional support. Call your local domestic abuse hotline, or if the threat is immediate, call 911.

Chapter 11: Building a Brand from Scratch

1. Are you able to adapt easily when things get sticky?

2. What is one dream project you have on your bucket list? What's keeping you from doing it? Is it a valid reason?

3. Do you have a hard time accepting anything that isn't

absolutely perfect? In what way can you lower your standards so that you can enjoy the work you do?

4. With regard to that dream project, go to YouTube or your local library and look up three books or videos on the topic. Read or watch them. What did you learn?

Chapter 12: Trolls and Insecurities

1. Do you ever feel intimidated by others on social media or afraid that you don't measure up in some way?

2. What unique message do you want to bring to the table?

3. Do you compare yourself with others and let that comparison get you down? Not just with social media, perhaps, but in anything? The way you decorate your house compared to a neighbor? The success you have at your day job compared to your friends in a small group? What are ways you can eliminate that comparison?

4. Who in your life can step up as your cheerleader and encourage you every moment of the way? Talk to them. Tell them about your goals and dreams.

5. Do you realize that you really are wonderfully and beautifully made? Do you believe it? If not, remind yourself that you are because God specifically made you, and just as no two fingerprints or snowflakes are alike, there is no one on earth exactly like you.

Chapter 13: Monetize Through Social Media

1. Of all the ways you can monetize on social media, what is the path that looks the most intriguing? Why?

2. Write down a list of steps to get you started on that path, and then go for it.

3. Do you have a media kit? If not, start working on one now.

4. Do you know who you want to work with? Research three brands you would love to collaborate with.

5. Draft an email request for collaboration, without necessarily sending it yet, preparing you for the day you take that step.

Chapter 14: Patience and Peace

1. When did you have patience for something you wanted, and how sweet was the moment when you received it?

2. Do you struggle with feeling content with your life and the things in it?

3. How can you practice slowing down and feeling at peace with your life in the present?

4. What do you think of the old saying, "A change in geography does not create a change in character"? How is this true with what you've experienced in your life or seen from others?

5. What are the most important things in your life that bring you joy?

Acknowledgments

My husband Daniel, what a whirlwind journey we have been on. From our days in the camper to our moments experiencing things neither of us ever thought possible—you have been a constant source of love, encouragement, and inspiration. You dream bigger than anyone I have ever known and through the good and the bad, the highs and the lows, there is no one I would rather have by my side. Thank you for believing in me and loving me through it all.

My beautiful children: Aisley, Ava, Amelia, and Crew. Though part of me wishes you would never grow up, I love you a gazillion lighting strikes and am so proud of you. I fought so hard for every single one of you and of all the blessings in my life, you are the ones I am most grateful for.

Our families: we are so blessed to have such a supportive and loving family. We love you all so much and are so grateful for you! My loving Nanny, your love for antiques and decor inspired a passion in me at such a young age. I wish you were alive to see what the spark you lit in me has flamed into.

My cowriter, Melissa Ferguson: it all started with one direct message. That conversation led to this book coming to life and I will forever owe you an enormous debt of gratitude. The countless Marco Polos and hours of conversations that resulted in this manuscript led to a friendship I will cherish forever. Thank you from the bottom of my heart.

Leslie Brown, our amazing photographer. You believed in us from the beginning and spoke so much encouragement into our hearts, giving freely of your time and love. You are so talented, and we are so grateful for you!

To my fabulous team at Thomas Nelson: Jenny Baumgartner, thank you for finding inspiration in my story and allowing me the opportunity to tell it to the world. I know none of this would be possible without you and you will forever have my deepest gratitude. Brigitta Nortker, your patience and wisdom in guiding this book to completion is truly appreciated! Lauren Langston Stewart, thank you for your guidance in developing our manuscript! To the marketing team: Rachel Tockstein, thank you for keeping us organized and on track in our marketing endeavors. Claire Drake, we appreciate all of your hard work! To the publicity team: Sara Broun, your enthusiasm is contagious, and I am so grateful for the opportunity to work with you! And to the art director: Kristina Juodenas, thank you for making our cover so beautiful!

My wonderful agent, Kimberly Whalen, thank you for guidance, wisdom, and expertise throughout this process.

Liz Marie Galven, I am incredibly grateful for the inspiration, support, and friendship you bring to my life. Thank you for giving of your time and energy to write such a thoughtful foreword.

To our TikTok and Instagram families: absolutely none of this would be possible without you. The love and support you have shown our family along our journey have changed our lives and we are eternally grateful to every single one of you.

notes

1. *Shall We Dance?*, directed by Peter Chelsom (Los Angeles, CA: Miramax, 2004).
2. Psalm 139:14.

About the Author

Noell Jett is the creative force behind the popular Jett Set Farmhouse, where she and her husband Daniel, along with their four children, share their lives, DIY tips, cleaning and organization hacks, recipes, homeschooling advice, and their home building journey with their millions of followers. They are currently building their second farmhouse in Saint Augustine, Florida.

Melissa Ferguson is the bestselling author of *The Dating Charade, The Cul-de-Sac War,* and *Meet Me in the Margins.* She lives in Tennessee with her husband and children in a farmhouse of their own and writes heartwarming romantic comedies that have been featured in multiple places including *The Hollywood Reporter, Travel + Leisure, Buzzfeed,* and *Woman's World.* She'd love for you to join her at @ourfriendlyfarmhouse and/or www.melissaferguson.com.